NEXT FALL

BY GEOFFREY NAUFFTS

DRAMATISTS
PLAY SERVICE
INC.

SPECIAL NOTE
Anyone receiving permission to produce NEXT FALL is required to give credit to the Author as sole and exclusive Author of the Play on the title page of all programs distributed in connection with performances of the Play and in all instances in which the title of the Play appears for purposes of advertising, publicizing or otherwise exploiting the Play and/or a production thereof. The name of the Author must appear on a separate line, in which no other name appears, immediately beneath the title and in size of type equal to 50% of the size of the largest, most prominent letter used for the title of the Play. No person, firm or entity may receive credit larger or more prominent than that accorded the Author. The following acknowledgment must appear on the title page in all programs distributed in connection with performances of the Play:

NEXT FALL was produced on Broadway by
Elton John and David Furnish, Barbara Manocherian, Richard Willis,
Tom Smedes, Carole L. Haber/Chase Mishkin, Ostar, Anthony Barrile,
Michael Palitz, Bob Boyett, James Spry/Catherine Schreiber,
Probo Productions, Roy Furman,
in association with Naked Angels.

In addition, if the music below is used in performances, the following acknowledgment must appear on the title page in all programs in size of type equal to that used for the production designers:

Sound Design and Original Music by John Gromada

SPECIAL NOTE ON MUSIC
A CD with cue sheet of the sound design and original music by John Gromada is available through the Play Service for $35.00, plus shipping and handling. The nonprofessional fee for the use of this music is $25.00 per performance.

2

AUTHOR'S NOTE

This is essentially a memory play; the entire action taking place during a twelve-hour period in the waiting room of an ICU. Transitions should be seamless, from present to past, and back to present again. A sense that the waiting room never quite disappears might be helpful to convey this. Characters, no matter what side of the equation, should be portrayed as intelligently as possible. Redneck behavior and proselytizing should be avoided at all cost. Though clichés are uttered, they are never uttered in cliché ways. In the end, these are six relatable human beings in search of some kind of grace. Humor is essential, particularly in the first act when the belief that Luke will pull through is high. Sentimentality is something to steer clear of throughout. Though things go from bad to worse in the second act, an active need to do what's best for Luke leaves everyone, with the exception of a few select moments, feeling a bit sideswiped and unable to express the true depths of their sadness.

NEXT FALL was given its world premiere by Naked Angels (Geoffrey Nauffts, Artistic Director; John Alexander, Managing Director; Andy Donald, Associate Artistic Director; Brittany O'Neill, Producer) at the Peter Jay Sharp Theater in New York City on June 3, 2009. The production then transferred to Broadway's Helen Hayes Theatre, opening on March 11, 2010. It was produced on Broadway by Elton John and David Furnish, Barbara Manocherian, Richard Willis, Tom Smedes, Carole L. Haber/Chase Mishkin Ostar, Anthony Barrile, Michael Palitz, Bob Boyett, James Spry/Catherine Schreiber, Probo Productions, Roy Furman in association with Naked Angels. Susan Mindell was the Executive Producer. It was directed by Sheryl Kaller; the set design was by Wilson Chin; the costume design was by Jess Goldstein; the lighting design was by Jeff Croiter; the original music and sound design were by John Gromada; and the stage manager was Charles Means. The cast was as follows:

ADAM .... Patrick Breen
HOLLY .... Maddie Corman
BRANDON .... Sean Dugan
LUKE .... Patrick Heusinger
ARLENE .... Connie Ray
BUTCH .... Cotter Smith

CHARACTERS

ADAM, 45, a substitute teacher

LUKE, 30, an aspiring actor

HOLLY, 35, a candle shop owner

BRANDON, 30, a property developer

ARLENE, 50, a divorcee

BUTCH, 55, a businessman

PLACE

Manhattan.

TIME

The action takes place in the present,
as well as the five-year period leading up to it.

In a moment, in the twinkling of an eye, at the last trumpet, for the trumpet shall sound, and the dead shall be raised incorruptible, and we shall be changed.

—1 Corinthians 15:52

No one's the devil, here. We're all just trying to get along.

—Anonymous

NEXT FALL

ACT ONE

Scene 1

In darkness we hear brakes squeal to a crashing halt, followed by a car horn stuck in a plaintive wail. The horn begins to sound like a trumpet's call before fading out.

A small waiting area off an ICU at a Jewish hospital. Mint green. Sterile. The low buzz of fluorescent lighting. There's a couch, two armchairs, a TV and a small coffee table holding a box of Kleenex and some magazines. A pair of doors upstage lead to a hallway that goes on forever.

Brandon sits, contemplatively thumbing the pages of an old book. Holly peruses a magazine next to him. She tosses it down with a sigh, and their eyes meet.

HOLLY. Weird, huh?

BRANDON. Yeah.

HOLLY. How quickly that rug gets pulled out from underneath you? *(A beat.)*

BRANDON. What rug?

HOLLY. Any rug. The proverbial rug. It's like, one minute you're doing the morning crossword, next thing you know, you're, well … here.

BRANDON. … Yeah. *(Arlene blows in like a tornado.)*

ARLENE. Here you go, hon. *(She hands Holly a cup of coffee.)* Black, right?

HOLLY. Perfect.

ARLENE. Wish I could drink it like that. I mean, I like my cream and sugar, don't get me wrong, but I like my thighs, too. Especially when they're not rubbing up against each other.

HOLLY. Thanks. *(Arlene plops down with her own coffee.)*

ARLENE. My dog is gonna strangle me, I swear. She's just gonna wrap her little paws around my neck and wring it.

HOLLY. You have a dog?

ARLENE. *(Nodding.)* My neighbor said she'd keep an eye on her, but ... She's Puerto Rican ... My dog, not the ... Well, my neighbor's Puerto Rican, too ... Chihuahua ... That's Puerto Rican, isn't it? Or is it Mexican?

BRANDON. Um ...

ARLENE. It's something Latin. She's got that temperament, you know? I've only had her a week, and already it's like we're in prison and I'm her bitch. Can't stand it when anyone comes near me. She gets all snarly and yappy. It's made us real popular at the dog park, let me tell you.

HOLLY. It's always the little ones.

ARLENE. Oh, she's a pain in my butt, she really is. But I love her, I do. Like a biscuit sandwich. Luke's dad thinks I've turned into one of those scary dog people. He threatened to call my shrink the other day when he found out how much I've been spending on chewy toys.

HOLLY. How's he doing?

ARLENE. Who?

HOLLY. Mister ...

ARLENE. Honeycut ... You can call him Butch. He's fine. Off spraying his spray, I bet. Makes him feel better.

HOLLY. I only know Luke by his stage name.

ARLENE. The stage name, right. I wouldn't bring that up around Butch. It's kind of a sore subject.

HOLLY. I think it was a union thing if that makes him feel any better.

ARLENE. Not really. *(She blows on her coffee.)* Now, Brandon, why do you look so familiar?

BRANDON. Luke's *Our Town* opening?

ARLENE. That's right. Lord, my mind's going. I can't remember a thing anymore.

BRANDON. At that sushi restaurant.

ARLENE. It's not so much my long term memory. That's pretty good. My short term's not bad either. It's just everything in between that's getting a little fuzzy ... Was I flapping my gums the whole night? Holding court?

BRANDON. You seemed to be enjoying yourself.

ARLENE. Of course, I was. You should've stuffed a nori roll in my mouth, Brandon. That's what you have to do, you know, or I'll go on for days.

BRANDON. I remember your turban being quite the topic of conversation.

ARLENE. Oh, no. With the nuts?

BRANDON. There were lots of squirrel jokes.

ARLENE. My friend Spike makes those. Uses raisins, too. Wheat Chex. M&Ms. Anything you find in a bag of trail mix, Spike uses it. It's called "outsider art." Because that's where it ought to be hung — outside — where no one has to look at it. We're not speaking any- more, Spike and me. I mean, what the heck was I thinking? *(A beat.)*

HOLLY. I wore a do-rag my last two years of high school.

ARLENE. A do what?

HOLLY. Rag? It holds your Jheri curl in place?

ARLENE. Shut up.

HOLLY. It's true. I have the prom pictures to prove it.

ARLENE. Good God, woman.

HOLLY. I wore a snood, too. One of those big yarn ones.

ARLENE. What the heck's a snood?

HOLLY. It's like a sweater for your hair?

ARLENE. No sir! How about you, Brandon? Any skeletons hang- ing in your closet?

BRANDON. Ties, I guess? I only wore red, white and blue ones when I worked in D.C.

ARLENE. Now, is that how you and Luke know each other, hon? D.C.?

BRANDON. Luke's the one who convinced me to move up here.

ARLENE. Well, that's Luke now, isn't it? Like Tom Sawyer with a can of whitewash. His daddy's the same way.

HOLLY. Brandon works for a big property developer. He's making more money than all of us.

ARLENE. Stop it.

BRANDON. It's hard to believe, but it's been a good couple of years, so ...

ARLENE. What about you two? How do you kids know each other? *(Holly and Brandon exchange a glance.)*
HOLLY. We don't really. We've met like, what, once or twice, right, Brandon?
BRANDON. Through Luke, yeah.
HOLLY. Luke works at my shop.
ARLENE. The candle store? That's yours?
HOLLY. Well, candles and cards and tchotchkes and things, yeah. We're expanding.
ARLENE. Chachis?
HOLLY. Tchotchkes.
ARLENE. Is that like bagels ... Something Jewish?
HOLLY. It's basically all the little, crappy things that clutter up your house. Knickknacks, I guess.
ARLENE. Okay, now you're speaking my language. My condo's like a chachi warehouse.
HOLLY. Tchotchke.
ARLENE. Huh?
HOLLY. Never mind. *(Holly sips her coffee.)*
ARLENE. From Capitol Hill to candles. No wonder his daddy's got high blood pressure.
HOLLY. Actually, candles are really in now.
ARLENE. Oh, I know, hon. I'm just teasing. I love candles. Luke sends me a different flavor for every holiday. Just the other day, I got my pumpkin spice.
HOLLY. That's our best seller. *(Laughter erupts in the hallway. It's eerie.)*
ARLENE. Someone's having a good time ... *(They listen for a moment. Arlene shifts gears.)* And, so Luke likes it up here? He's having a nice life in New York?
HOLLY. He loves it.
ARLENE. I keep waiting to see his face on TV again. There was that commercial he did a while back. For computers, was it? Or cell phones?
BRANDON. DSL.
ARLENE. Okay, see, now I have no idea what that is, either. You must think I'm some kind of hillbilly, twankin' my banjo down there in the boonies somewhere.
HOLLY. I don't know what it is either ... and I have it.
ARLENE. I enjoyed that musical he was in a while back.

HOLLY. Who knew Luke could sing?

ARLENE. Like an angel … But my favorite still, Brandon, was that *Our Town*.

BRANDON. Yeah.

ARLENE. Luke was just terrific in that. Especially when the girl died. He was so believable.

HOLLY. Yeah, the acting thing's been going really well for him.

ARLENE. And he still has all that time to sell candles. *(Butch enters, with medical forms.)*

BUTCH. Idiots.

ARLENE. What now, Butch?

BUTCH. The taxi driver's uninsured.

ARLENE. Oh, for Pete's sake.

BUTCH. No green card, either.

ARLENE. Would you leave that poor man alone! He's traumatized enough as it is.

BUTCH. Who lets these jackasses across the border, that's what I want to know. He didn't just go through the red light. He ran right up on the sidewalk.

ARLENE. It was an accident.

BUTCH. And don't get me started with the ambulance driver.

ARLENE. Pay no attention to him, you all. He hasn't been here an hour, and he's already tried to have two interns and a security guard fired.

BUTCH. Well, they were dumb, too.

ARLENE. It's called a Napoleon complex.

BUTCH. Napoleon was short.

ARLENE. Ought to see if we can't get you a shot for that while we're here, hon.

BUTCH. I'm keeping a list. That's what I'm gonna do.

ARLENE. Oh, that's helpful, Butch. That's real constructive.

BUTCH. I'll sue the whole damn city if I have to.

ARLENE. Would you hush?! *(Butch sits, frustrated.)*

BUTCH. Knuckleheads.

ARLENE. Have you called Lynn yet?

BUTCH. I can't deal with Lynn right now.

ARLENE. Well, neither can I, and I'm the one she keeps speed dialing.

BUTCH. I told you not to give her your damn cell phone number.

ARLENE. *(To Holly.)* Luke's stepmom.

13

HOLLY. Oh. I thought you were his …

ARLENE. Oh, no, hon. Lynn did a lot of the rearing, but I'm the real deal. Poor thing had a brow lift and a tummy tuck yesterday, can you imagine? And then this happens? She's been calling every half hour in a complete Vicodin haze, bless her heart. Can't understand a word she's saying. *(To Butch.)* Of course, she's got the housekeeper and the personal trainer five times a week, so I can't feel too bad for her.

BUTCH. You coulda had that if you'd behaved yourself.

ARLENE. How about Ben? Have you reached Ben yet?

BUTCH. My phone's not getting any service.

ARLENE. Well, here, try mine. *(Arlene fishes a cell phone out of her coat pocket and hands it over.)* Luke's brother. He's a sophomore at Georgia Tech.

BUTCH. An engineering major.

ARLENE. He's pledging a fraternity today.

BUTCH. Nuclear engineering. Got a 3.9 last semester.

ARLENE. Sweet kid.

BUTCH. He's gonna work for NASA someday. *(Into the phone.)* Ben, it's your dad again. Give me a call as soon as you get this, son. It's important. *(He hangs the phone up and hands it back, the reality of the situation hitting them all. Arlene sticks it back in her coat pocket, and switches gears.)*

ARLENE. That anaesthesiologist seems nice, Holly. The one with the hook nose and the beanie. And cute, too. Are you single?

HOLLY. Um …

ARLENE. I'll introduce you later on. After Luke wakes up. So glad they brought him to a Jewish hospital.

BUTCH. Arlene …

ARLENE. We're lucky, that's all. They make great doctors. Accountants, too.

BUTCH. Christ on a Christmas tree …

ARLENE. You clip those curlicue things off the side of his head, he'd look just like George Clooney, wouldn't he, Holly?

BUTCH. Arlene, why don't you be still and muzzle it for a while. *(Adam enters, wet and exhausted.)*

HOLLY. Adam?!

ADAM. Oh, my God. *(He makes a beeline for the coat rack.)*

HOLLY. I thought your flight was canceled.

ADAM. You wouldn't believe the hoops I had to jump through to get here. *(Holly tries to cut him off at the pass.)*

HOLLY. This is Adam, everybody.

ADAM. We sat on the tarmac for like two hours.

HOLLY. I didn't think you were gonna make it in tonight, sweetie.

ADAM. I'm starving. All I've had to eat today is like three Bloody Marys and a Cinnabon. *(He hangs his wet coat up and turns, paralyzed, when he sees Arlene and the rest of the gang staring at him.)*

ARLENE. Hi there.

HOLLY. This is Arlene, Adam. Luke's mom.

ARLENE. Nice to meet you.

HOLLY. And you know Brandon.

BRANDON. Hey …

HOLLY. Brandon was the first one to get here.

BRANDON. I only live a couple blocks away, so …

ADAM. You moved?

BRANDON. A few months ago … Yeah.

HOLLY. And Luke's dad.

ARLENE. Stand up, Butch. Have some manners.

ADAM. We've met.

BUTCH. We have? *(Holly pushes Adam towards a chair.)*

HOLLY. Why don't you have a seat, sweetie?

ADAM. Where is he?

HOLLY. Just out of surgery. He was in there for, like, five hours.

ADAM. Can I see him?

HOLLY. They want us to hold off for a while.

ADAM. Can't I just stick my head in?

HOLLY. He's still in the coma. *(Adam sinks into a chair, the weight of it all finally hitting him.)* Adam was just at his high school reunion. He must be feeling like we were when we first got here. It's a little overwhelming, isn't it, sweetie?

ADAM. He's gonna be okay though, right?

HOLLY. Of course, he is.

ADAM. I mean, that's what they're saying, isn't it?

ARLENE. Well, now, Butch, you were the last one to speak to the surgeon, sweetheart. What did he have to say?

BUTCH. He said my boy's got fight in him.

ARLENE. He certainly does. We were just talking about that, weren't we, Brandon? Pluck. That's what we called it growing up.

BUTCH. Pluck?

ARLENE. *(Snippy.)* Yes, pluck, Butch. That's what we called it.

Luke's got a ton of it. What else did he say? *(A beat.)*
BUTCH. He's gonna need it. *(Adam goes pale as the room spins all around him.)*

Scene 2

Lights up on a rooftop. Five years earlier. Adam, pale and sweaty, is trying to catch his breath. Luke, wearing a white shirt and black pants, steps out and hands over a glass of water.

LUKE. Here you go. *(Adam takes a huge gulp.)*
ADAM. Thanks.
LUKE. Sorry about the Heimlich.
ADAM. Don't worry about it.
LUKE. I thought you were choking.
ADAM. I think it was more of an arrythmia thing. *(He downs the rest of the water and hands the glass back.)* Is the roof spinning or is it just me?
LUKE. Have you tried sticking your arms in the air?
ADAM. You think?
LUKE. I saw it on TV once. Some doctor show. *(Adam sticks his arms in the air.)* How's that feel?
ADAM. Like I'm under arrest.
LUKE. Might have been a cop show. *(Adam lowers his arms and sinks to the floor.)*
ADAM. I think maybe if I just sit here for a minute.
LUKE. Some party, huh?
ADAM. Fabulous.
LUKE. Who's anniversary is it anyway?
ADAM. My friend Holly's.
LUKE. The large woman?
ADAM. She's fat. You can say it ... No, not her. That's a friend of hers.
LUKE. Oh, sorry. Didn't mean to ...
ADAM. That's okay. She wasn't always like that, apparently.
LUKE. You can tell. Some people just seem like they've been fat

their whole lives, you know? Like they're used to it. But she looks like it kinda snuck up on her out of nowhere ... And suddenly, there she was. This fat fatty.

ADAM. What happened to large?

LUKE. Like she woke up one morning in someone else's skin.

ADAM. Yeah, well, she's on the road to recovery now, so ...

LUKE. What do you mean?

ADAM. It's not a real anniversary down there. It's a twelve-step thing.

LUKE. Twelve-step? You mean, like, AA?

ADAM. Yeah, only it's OA.

LUKE. OA?

ADAM. Overeaters Anonymous.

LUKE. Oh, I get it.

ADAM. Listen, thanks for the water, but I think I can take it from here. *(Luke reaches out his hand.)*

LUKE. We haven't officially met yet.

ADAM. You gotta be kidding, I practically threw up on you.

LUKE. I'm Luke. *(Adam shakes his hand, tentatively.)*

ADAM. Adam.

LUKE. Nice to meet you, Adam. So what do *you* do?

ADAM. *(Off guard.)* What do *I* do?

LUKE. Yeah.

ADAM. Like in life?

LUKE. Is that a trick question?

ADAM. Uh ...

LUKE. Like, me? I'm an actor.

ADAM. No kidding?

LUKE. Is it that obvious?

ADAM. The white shirt. The black pants ... The serving tray.

LUKE. Okay, I'm an aspiring actor. I'm not really making any money at it yet, so I guess, technically, I'm a cater waiter.

ADAM. Gotcha.

LUKE. Not for long though. *(Luke digs a postcard out of his pocket and hands it over.)*

ADAM. What's this?

LUKE. A show I'm working on. We go up next week.

ADAM. Oh ... Well, break a leg.

LUKE. I wanted the part of George, but I'm the Stage Manager.

ADAM. Well, we all have to start somewhere. *(Adam sticks it in his pocket.)*

LUKE. What about you?

ADAM. Me? We're back to me again?

LUKE. Are you like a Wall Street guy? An accountant, maybe?

ADAM. An accountant? I look like an accountant?

LUKE. An ad exec? I don't know. A sous chef?

ADAM. No, none of those.

LUKE. Come on, help me out here.

ADAM. *(Hitting a nerve.)* I'm not so sure anymore. *(Luke joins him on the floor.)*

LUKE. Well, what would you like to do?

ADAM. What would I like to do?

LUKE. You're a vamper.

ADAM. A what?

LUKE. You keep repeating the question. That's what I always do when I'm not sure how to answer.

ADAM. *(Considering.)* What would I like to do?

LUKE. See? You did it again.

ADAM. I'm thinking. Give me a sec. *(Adam leans his head back, searching for an answer.)* I read about this experiment once, they took a newborn and stuck it in a room with no light, no love, no stimuli, and just left it. They'd come in, every so often, and feed it through some kind of tube, you know, but it basically had no human contact whatsoever.

LUKE. That's criminal.

ADAM. Maybe I'm getting it wrong. Maybe it wasn't a newborn. Maybe it was a mouse. Yeah, I think that's what it was. A baby mouse.

LUKE. Still.

ADAM. Anyway, that's how they raised the little rodent. And sure enough, he grew up to be, like, a complete vegetable. When they finally threw him into a tank with some other mice, he wouldn't even move.

LUKE. Sad.

ADAM. Just sat in the corner and shook.

LUKE. And your point is …

ADAM. You tell someone "no" long enough, they start believing it. Does that answer your question?

LUKE. Not really. But we can move on to the next topic.

ADAM. I guess I'm a candle salesman.

LUKE. There you go.

ADAM. That's what I do.

LUKE. That wasn't so hard.

ADAM. Jesus, how did I wind up being that?

LUKE. You can change your mind if you like.

ADAM. No, I'm a candle salesman.

LUKE. Good for you.

ADAM. Yup, I sell candles.

LUKE. Okay, easy now.

ADAM. It's just the first time I've ever really admitted it out loud.

LUKE. And how does it feel?

ADAM. Terrible. I don't care if I ever sell another pumpkin-scented anything for as long as I live.

LUKE. I hate pumpkin.

HOLLY. Adam! *(Holly appears from the party below.)*

ADAM. Sorry.

HOLLY. It was quirky for, like, ten minutes, now it's just rude.

ADAM. I said I'm sorry.

HOLLY. Well, get back down there. It's my anniversary.

ADAM. I can't.

HOLLY. What do you mean you can't?

ADAM. The air. There's like a pall down there.

HOLLY. A pall?

ADAM. A heaviness, yeah. I don't know. Everyone just seems so … hungry.

HOLLY. You done, Shecky?

ADAM. What happened to all those past-life regression weirdos you used to hang out with? At least those people knew how to party. *(Holly sits, as it all comes clear.)*

HOLLY. It's Belinda, isn't it?

ADAM. Who?

HOLLY. That's what this is all about.

ADAM. Absolutely not.

HOLLY. It's just a book, sweetie.

ADAM. A best-selling book. She's making a fortune.

HOLLY. Well, good for her. We should all be so lucky.

ADAM. They're making a movie of it, too.

HOLLY. That's ridiculous.

ADAM. No, it's not. There's a huge bidding war, apparently.

HOLLY. It's a book on breast feeding, Adam.

ADAM. I'd pay to see that.

HOLLY. Okay, I'm leaving now. *(She starts offstage.)*

ADAM. I'm a candle salesman, Holly. *(She stops and turns.)*

HOLLY. What?

ADAM. I'm a forty-year-old candle salesman.

HOLLY. What are you talking about?

ADAM. That's just not what I thought I'd be at this point in my life.

HOLLY. Oh, for fuck sake.

ADAM. When you hired me, it was to help you get through the holiday season.

HOLLY. So?

ADAM. That was six years ago. *(A beat.)* I don't want to end up like your friend downstairs.

HOLLY. Which one?

ADAM. Whats-her-name, the middle aged fat one who sells bongs in the smoke shop around the corner.

HOLLY. Rachel?

ADAM. The one who looks like she cries in her closet.

HOLLY. She's nice.

ADAM. That's not what I want. *(Another beat.)*

HOLLY. Well, I sell candles, too.

ADAM. You own the shop, Holly. You're a shop owner. There's a big difference. Plus, you're not forty.

HOLLY. Neither are you.

ADAM. Yes, I am.

HOLLY. You're forty?

ADAM. Uh-huh.

HOLLY. You've been lying about your age the whole time I've known you?

ADAM. Yes.

HOLLY. *(Processing for a moment.)* Well, you're not fat.

ADAM. My body may not be, but my soul is.

HOLLY. Okay, now I'm really leaving. *(Adam stands.)*

ADAM. I want more, Holly.

HOLLY. There is more, Adam. There's cake. And we want to watch you eat it.

ADAM. I'm serious! I'll give you a couple more weeks.

HOLLY. *(Realizing he's serious.)* So, what, you're quitting? Great. Who's gonna help me unload that huge crate of Diptyques we just got in? You're the only one who knows how to pronounce those freakin' things.

ADAM. You'll find someone else.

HOLLY. *(To Luke.)* Hey, handsome, wanna sell candles?

LUKE. Is that better than cater-waitering?

HOLLY. Way better. Talk to me on your way out. I'll hook you up.

LUKE. Cool.

HOLLY. *(Back to Adam.)* You feel better?

ADAM. A little ... You?

HOLLY. Fuck, no. I'm starving.

ADAM. Then have a piece of cake, Holly. Have two. You don't have an eating disorder.

HOLLY. You don't get it, do you?

ADAM. Get what? *(She shakes her head and starts off.)*

HOLLY. Okay, five more minutes, then I'm calling the guys with the straitjacket.

ADAM. Love you.

HOLLY. Yeah, yeah, yeah. *(And she's gone. Adam blots his forehead.)*

LUKE. Wow ...

ADAM. Sorry about that.

LUKE. Was that like a mid-life crisis, or something?

ADAM. Mid-life crisis? No ... What makes you say that?

LUKE. You quit your job and you're forty. *(Adam clutches his heart and starts pacing.)*

ADAM. I think it's happening again.

LUKE. Maybe you should try sticking your head between your legs?

ADAM. How about I stick it back up my ass? Where it's been for the past six years. *(He wanders over to the ledge and looks at the street below.)* She went to school with me. Belinda. The girl with the book.

LUKE. Oh.

ADAM. We were in the same writing program.

LUKE. I get it.

ADAM. I was the one with all the promise, and she was the one destined to ...

LUKE. ... write books on breastfeeding?

ADAM. I guess ... *(Luke sidles up next to him.)*

LUKE. I have a confession to make.

21

ADAM. What's that?

LUKE. I didn't really think you were choking when I gave you the Heimlich.

ADAM. No?

LUKE. I just wanted to get my arms around you. You looked so cute all doubled over like that.

ADAM. You should see me when I think I'm passing a kidney stone. *(Luke moves a little closer.)*

ADAM. We better get back down there.

LUKE. How about grabbing a drink later?

ADAM. I don't think so.

LUKE. Why not?

ADAM. Well, I could be your grandfather, for one.

LUKE. Okay, now you're really making me horny. *(Luke flashes him a killer grin, then exits. Adam takes out the postcard, hopeful.)*

Scene 3

The waiting room. Holly peruses a Newsweek *magazine. Brandon talks on his cell phone.*

BRANDON. No, the 220 Rivington offer is way too low … Look, I'm gonna be able to give this my full attention tomorrow. Could you please deal with it for now? … It's email, just pretend you're me. Thanks. *(He hangs up and looks at Holly.)*

HOLLY. They found a new missing link.

BRANDON. Huh?

HOLLY. In Ethiopia. This one's sixty thousand years older than the last one … That's encouraging. *(Adam enters with a cup of coffee.)*

ADAM. Well, my luggage arrived safely.

HOLLY. Thank God.

ADAM. In Pittsburgh.

HOLLY. Pittsburgh?

ADAM. Don't ask. *(He plops down on the couch, exhausted.)* God, that was awkward.

HOLLY. I thought you handled it pretty well.

ADAM. Are you kidding, it was a train wreck.

HOLLY. You're right.

ADAM. And you were the conductor.

HOLLY. Butch sure is a pistol.

ADAM. Yeah, and I'm sure he owns several, too.

HOLLY. He's way sexier than I imagined.

ADAM. I'm ignoring you.

HOLLY. He's just not as straitlaced as I thought he'd be. I expected him to look more like one of those TV preacher guys.

ADAM. Yeah, well, you don't see me in a thong on a float, but I'm still a fag.

HOLLY. True.

ADAM. God, I hate hospitals. It'll be a miracle if one of us doesn't leave here with a staph infection. Where are they, anyway? *(Holly and Brandon exchange a glance.)*

BRANDON. With Luke.

ADAM. What?

HOLLY. The surgeon said it was okay, sweetie.

ADAM. When?

HOLLY. Like ten, fifteen minutes ago.

ADAM. Why didn't anyone come get me? *(Adam rises, incredulous, and starts off.)*

BRANDON. Family only, Adam. *(Adam stops in his tracks.)*

ADAM. What?

BRANDON. They asked that it be family only.

ADAM. Who did?

BRANDON. The surgeon.

HOLLY. For now, sweetie. He seemed pretty adamant.

ADAM. Family only?

HOLLY. I don't think they can have too many people in the room. He just went through major surgery.

ADAM. Yeah, well, I'm not people, Holly.

HOLLY. I know.

ADAM. Who do you think he's been living with for the past four years?

HOLLY. I know, Adam. I know.

BRANDON. But it's not like they're strangers.

ADAM. Excuse me?

BRANDON. They said family only for now, so his parents went in. I mean …

ADAM. Okay, got it, Brandon. We know whose side you're on.

BRANDON. I'm not on anyone's side.

HOLLY. He's not, Adam. He's really not.

BRANDON. I just don't think this is the time to be getting all bent out of shape about it.

ADAM. I'm not getting … *(To Holly.)* Am I bent out of shape?

BRANDON. It's not about you right now. That's all I'm saying. It's not about any of us.

ADAM. What are you talking about?

HOLLY. Guys —

BRANDON. Luke needs us, Adam. He needs all of us together.

ADAM. You don't think I know that?

BRANDON. I'm not gonna argue with you.

ADAM. I am family, Brandon! I don't care what anyone says. I'm going in there! *(He starts off again. Holly chases after him.)*

HOLLY. But they don't know about you, sweetie.

ADAM. Oh, believe me, I'm well aware of that.

HOLLY. For a reason. *(He stops and turns.)* There's a reason Luke's never told them.

ADAM. Yeah, because he's a wimp. He's a scared little coward who should've told them a long time ago.

HOLLY. That may be, but —

ADAM. What, Holly? What?

HOLLY. I'm not sure it's your place to tell.

ADAM. Oh, and whose place would it be?

HOLLY. Luke's. *(A beat.)* Just think about it for a minute, that's all I'm asking. When Luke wakes up. Is that really what he needs to deal with? On top of everything else? *(Butch enters, sensing the tension.)*

BUTCH. Everything okay in here?

HOLLY. We're fine, aren't we, guys?

BRANDON. I am.

HOLLY. How's Luke doing?

BUTCH. Alright, I guess. They had to clear us out of the room for a bit.

HOLLY. What for?

BUTCH. More tests.

HOLLY. Okay.

BUTCH. They've got some monitor thing bolted to his head. Specialists marching in and out every five minutes. It's hard to keep track of what all's going on in there.

HOLLY. I'm sure. *(Butch sits on the couch and pulls out his cell phone.)*

BUTCH. They had to remove a piece of his skull.

HOLLY. His ...

BUTCH. It's common, I guess. Because of the swelling. Epidural hematoma. That's what they're calling it.

HOLLY. Okay ...

BUTCH. Something about his fall. After the cab hit. The timing of it all. The way his head struck the pavement. You wouldn't have known anything was wrong when they first brought him in. That's what the nurse told us. It was just like he was sleeping.

HOLLY. Is there anything we can do?

BUTCH. Just sit tight. Like the surgeon said. He doesn't seem quite as inept as the rest of the folks around here. *(Butch starts dialing.)*

ADAM. *(Trying to be polite.)* And so this ... um ... The family-only request ... How long do you think that will, you know, be in effect?

BUTCH. Not sure.

ADAM. Hours? Minutes? Days? What?

HOLLY. Adam ...

ADAM. I'm just ... We'd like to see him, right, guys? Even for a second.

HOLLY. We're just feeling a little out of the loop, is all.

BUTCH. Well, they can't have us clogging up the room. They need to be able to get in and out of there and do whatever it is they do. *(Snapping phone shut.)* Shoot, still no service. *(Butch grabs Arlene's purse and starts digging through it.)*

ADAM. So, what's next then? Assuming all goes smoothly.

BUTCH. Next? I don't know. Physical therapy, I suppose. Rehabilitation.

ADAM. And how much of that do they think he'll need?

BUTCH. They, who?

ADAM. The surgeons, they? I don't know. Whoever's in charge?

HOLLY. Sweetie ...

ADAM. Months? A year, maybe? Longer?

BUTCH. Nobody's saying much of anything right now, son. We probably won't know what's what for sure until we get him back home.

HOLLY. Home?

BUTCH. There's a brand new facility just outside Tallahassee.

State of the art, from what I hear, and booked up like a five-star hotel. I've got a couple strings I can pull. See if we can't get him in there. *(Butch moves on to Arlene's coat.)*

ADAM. Is that wise?

BUTCH. Wise?

ADAM. Transporting him like that? I mean, he just went through major surgery.

BUTCH. I'm not sure if it's wise or not, but that's what I'm gonna do.

ADAM. It's just … Head trauma can be pretty serious, from what I understand. Has anyone determined if there's been any …

BUTCH. No one's determined anything yet. *(He pulls out a bottle of pills and examines the label.)* We all just have to sit tight. *(A look of disappointment crosses his face, then he pockets them.)* And try not to worry.

Scene 4

Adam's apartment. Five years earlier. Luke, in his boxers, prepares breakfast.

LUKE. Wait 'til you taste these tomatoes. They're fierce.

ADAM. *(Offstage.)* Fierce? Tomatoes aren't fierce. Lions are. Whitney Houston is. Tomatoes are just … tomatoes.

LUKE. Where you been, Grandpa? Whitney Houston hasn't been fierce in years. She's a crackhead. *(Adam enters in his boxers with a big smile on his face.)*

ADAM. I know I said it already, but you were really amazing last night.

LUKE. You mean it?

ADAM. When you told me you were the Stage Manager, I didn't realize it was an actual part.

LUKE. The lead part.

ADAM. You were brilliant. The whole production was. I cried.

LUKE. I know, I heard you … Everyone in the audience heard you.

ADAM. I'm having a mid-life crisis. It was cathartic. *(Adam sits in front of a plate of eggs.)* Looks delicious.

LUKE. It's the best I could do with what you had in your fridge.

ADAM. I didn't even know I had a fridge.

LUKE. Dig in before it gets cold.

ADAM. I think the only one who cried more than me was that weird lady in the turban.

LUKE. That was my mother.

ADAM. Did I say weird? I meant eccentric.

LUKE. Turbans are her thing right now. Last year it was tracksuits. The year before it was chunky jewelry. *(Adam starts eating.)*

ADAM. And your dad?

LUKE. He was a no-show. Still mad I dropped out of law school, I guess. It's just as well. He gets kind of cranky whenever he and my mom are in the same room together. The "Arlene Show" can be a little exhausting after twenty years.

ADAM. How long have they been divorced?

LUKE. Twenty years. He kind of turned his life around after they split up. It was just me and him for a while there. I was like his little security blanket. He dragged me everywhere.

ADAM. So, that must have been challenging. Your folks divorcing when you were so young.

LUKE. I was just glad the craziness was over.

ADAM. What kind of crazy?

LUKE. Like waking up in the middle of the night to a house full of pot smoke, Pink Floyd on the stereo, the front door wide open and nobody in sight.

ADAM. Sounds like my entire four years of college.

LUKE. Well, it's no fun when you're in kindergarten, trust me. To this day, the smell of patchouli oil makes me weep. *(Adam watches, curiously, as Luke closes his eyes for a moment, prays, then opens them again and digs in.)*

ADAM. What was that?

LUKE. What was what?

ADAM. Where'd you go just then?

LUKE. I was praying.

ADAM. You mean, crystals and chakras? Like a Deepak Chopra kind of thing?

LUKE. Not really.

ADAM. Then, who were you praying to?

LUKE. God.

ADAM. Oh. *(The honeymoon just ended.)*

LUKE. Yum.

ADAM. Is that an everyday occurrence?

LUKE. Pretty much.

ADAM. So, you're what, then … You're — a …

LUKE. Christian.

ADAM. Okay. *(Adam tries to proceed with breakfast as usual.)*

LUKE. Does that freak you out?

ADAM. Does it freak me out?

LUKE. Yeah.

ADAM. Why would it freak me out?

LUKE. No reason … Why? What are you?

ADAM. What am I?

LUKE. Besides a vamper.

ADAM. Nothing … I don't know. I didn't really grow up with a religion. *(Luke stabs a tomato and pops it in his mouth.)*

LUKE. These tomatoes are fierce. I don't care what you say. *(Adam looks at him, suspiciously.)*

ADAM. You're gay though, right?

LUKE. Uh … whose lips do you think you were mackin' on all night?

ADAM. I know, but don't Christians consider that a sin?

LUKE. Uh-huh.

ADAM. So, how does that work, then?

LUKE. How does what work?

ADAM. Being gay and.. you know …

LUKE. This is gonna be a problem, isn't it?

ADAM. No … I'm … I just …

LUKE. We're all sinners, Adam. We all struggle with one thing or another. This one just happens to be mine.

ADAM. Do you atone, then? Is that what you do?

LUKE. You really want to talk about this?

ADAM. Sure. *(Luke indulges him.)*

LUKE. You accept Christ as the Son of God. That He died on the cross for all your sins.

ADAM. That's it?

LUKE. Pretty much.

ADAM. And you'll go to heaven?

LUKE. If you believe. If you truly believe.

ADAM. And you do?

LUKE. Uh-huh. *(Luke refills Adam's coffee.)*

ADAM. Then how come you continue to sin? I mean, and don't get me wrong, that was some amazing sinning we just did, I look forward to more, but you sinned a lot. You sinned more than I did.

LUKE. I was hoping we could sin again after breakfast.

ADAM. You didn't answer my question.

LUKE. It's human nature, Adam. We can't escape it. But as long as you've accepted Christ … *(A beat.)*

ADAM. Is that why you didn't introduce me to your mom last night?

LUKE. I didn't?

ADAM. Nope.

LUKE. Might have had a little something to do with it. *(Luke rises and starts clearing the table.)*

ADAM. So, let me see if I got this right. I'm assuming sin is sin. And if your sin is having sex with men, and my sin is, say, *killing* men who have sex with men, then as long as I've accepted Christ as my Savior, I'll go to heaven with you?

LUKE. Killing men who have sex with men? You mean, like Jeffrey Dahmer?

ADAM. Yeah … Well, no. Because he killed them, then he ate them. Plus, he had sex with them too, so no, not him.

LUKE. Like who, then?

ADAM. The guys who killed Matthew Shepard. *(A beat.)*

LUKE. Technically, yes.

ADAM. Not only that, but I can continue to kill men who have sex with men, much as you continue to have sex with them, every day for the rest of my life, and still go to heaven?

LUKE. Well …

ADAM. It's just a hypothesis.

LUKE. I know it sounds terrible, but … yes.

ADAM. Huh. *(Can't quite let it go.)* So, then, if Matthew Shepard hadn't accepted Christ before he died, he's in hell, and his killers who, say, have, are going to heaven? Is that what you're saying? *(Luke stands there with his arms full.)*

LUKE. Can we change the subject?

Scene 5

Adam and Luke's new apartment. A year later. Holly, Chinese food and a housewarming gift in hand, stands amid a stack of unopened boxes as Luke pries something off the door frame.

HOLLY. And I thought my place was small.

ADAM. *(Offstage.)* I told you.

LUKE. Please don't get him started.

HOLLY. I just don't know where you're gonna put everything.

ADAM. *(Offstage.)* I like my old place better.

LUKE. Would you relax. *(Adam enters with a bottle of wine and two glasses.)*

ADAM. That kitchen is minuscule.

LUKE. Wait 'til I unpack everything and put it in its place. It'll look like a palace.

ADAM. What are you doing?

LUKE. Trying to get this thing off.

ADAM. What thing?

HOLLY. The mezuzah.

LUKE. Ma-wha-wha?

ADAM. Mezuzah. It keeps evil spirits out of New York apartments.

HOLLY. Actually, I think it protects your first born from being slaughtered.

LUKE. We don't have a first born.

ADAM. It's good luck, babe.

LUKE. It's ugly.

ADAM. Luke!

LUKE. Alright, already … Jeez. *(Luke rolls his eyes and pockets his screwdriver.)* I don't see how a little metal thing's gonna ward off evil spirits anyway.

ADAM. Yeah, well, I don't see how a golden trumpet's gonna signal the end of the world, so we're even. *(Luke disappears into the kitchen. Adam pours the wine.)* He literally believes that, you know. That people are gonna just start floating up to heaven.

LUKE. *(Offstage.)* I never said "float."

ADAM. That, like, Doc Severinsen, or some other dead trumpeter, is gonna blow his horn three times —

HOLLY. Gabriel.

ADAM. Yeah, him. And in the blink of an eye —

LUKE. *(Offstage.)* Twinkling.

ADAM. Whatever.

LUKE. *(Offstage.)* Get it right, sister.

ADAM. All believers will just disappear.

LUKE. *(Offstage.)* It's true. *(A beat.)*

HOLLY. Doc Severinsen is dead? *(Luke reenters.)*

ADAM. You should have heard him on the phone this morning. Giggling with his friend Jill.

HOLLY. Who's Jill, the beard?

LUKE. She's more like a soul patch.

ADAM. Hysterically laughing about all the wacky things people will be in the middle of when it happens. Tickled to death at the thought of me being on a plane with a Christian pilot, because the plane will crash and I'll go down with it. *(Luke takes a sip of Adam's wine and giggles.)* See? This is funny to him.

LUKE. This is the thirty-nine-dollar bottle of merlot we just bought?

ADAM. It was running low, so I mixed in a little of our ten-dollar bottle.

LUKE. So, it's a twenty-nine-dollar bottle now.

ADAM. It's woody … muddy … shitty. Just drink it. *(Holly raises her glass.)*

HOLLY. Cheers, guys. To your new place.

ADAM. Salut. *(They clink glasses.)*

HOLLY. And a little something … *(Holly pulls an orange candle out of her gift bag.)*

LUKE. Look, babe, it's pumpkin.

HOLLY. Didn't wanna come empty handed.

LUKE. It's sweet, thank you. *(Luke gives Holly a kiss and gets back to work.)*

HOLLY. So, you really think this thing's gonna happen, Luke?

LUKE. Uh-huh.

HOLLY. Like, in our lifetime?

LUKE. Maybe.

ADAM. And he and all his cohorts will float, or fly, or "beam," or whatever, up to heaven while the rest of us go to hell.

LUKE. That's not exactly how it works.

ADAM. All the agnostics and atheists. The Muslims and the Buddhists. The Hindus. The Jews. Three quarters of the world's population, all going to hell.

HOLLY. You mean, I'll finally get a decent apartment?

ADAM. No, you're going too, missy.

HOLLY. What about David? *(Holly checks out the kitchen.)*

ADAM. That asshole? You're still obsessing over him?

HOLLY. *(Offstage.)* He's a Scientologist.

ADAM. Especially him. *(She reenters.)* Anyone who doesn't truly believe.

HOLLY. Even the Mongolian goatherder?

LUKE. The Mongolian who?

ADAM. *(Singing.) High on a hill lived a Mongolian goatherder …*

HOLLY. You know, the guy who's been nothing but saintly to his family and fellow villagers his whole life. Toiling in the fields, tending his flock. Who's never even heard of Jesus. Is he going, too? Or his infant son, who can't even crawl yet? Or Rachel?

LUKE. The bong lady?

HOLLY. Her last name's Rosenberg. They're all gonna burn?

LUKE. Not the goatherder and his son.

HOLLY. Why not?

LUKE. Infants and retarded people are exempt.

ADAM. She said Mongolian, not mongoloid. *(A beat.)*

LUKE. Oh … Then, yeah. He'll burn with Rachel … Unless, of course, you know …

HOLLY. But what if you have your own set of beliefs? Beliefs that are equally as valid?

LUKE. I just know it's going to happen, you guys. It's kind of hard to explain.

ADAM. Try us. *(Luke engages.)*

LUKE. It's like … Imagine if you were a cancer patient, and they discovered a cure, but you're so pissed off you got sick in the first place, you refuse to take it and you die.

ADAM. I have no idea what he's talking about.

HOLLY. Going to hell is cancer, bozo. And Jesus is the pill.

LUKE. Like that, yeah.

ADAM. But I don't believe in hell, so why should I care whether I burn in it?

LUKE. Because I do! *(Luke tears a box open.)*

ADAM. Don't get defensive, babe.

LUKE. Whatever.

ADAM. Tell her about the seven years.

LUKE. I'm not talking about this anymore.

HOLLY. What seven years?

ADAM. Apparently, there's a seven-year period when we'll all get a chance to, you know, swallow the pill.

HOLLY. I thought everything happens in the twinkling of an eye.

ADAM. That's how long it'll take them to disappear, but the rest of us get seven more years before you-know-who arrives.

HOLLY. Mel Gibson?

ADAM. Close enough.

HOLLY. Well, I tell you what, Luke. If a third of the world's population suddenly disappears, I guarantee you, we'll accept Jesus. And it won't take seven years, it'll take more like seven seconds.

ADAM. Amen to that. *(Adam and Holly clink glasses.)*

LUKE. But what if you die before it happens? *(A sobering moment.)*

HOLLY. Wait a minute. What?

ADAM. He's afraid I'll die before I get a chance to, you know, "accept Christ," and then we won't be able to be in the afterlife together.

HOLLY. That's so sad.

ADAM. Not really. We're not allowed to be gay there, so what difference does it make?

HOLLY. That's true.

ADAM. No pets, either.

HOLLY. Sounds like my last co-op meeting. *(Luke drops a box on the floor, and lays into Adam.)*

LUKE. Why are you mocking me?

ADAM. I'm not mocking you.

LUKE. Yes, you are, Adam. You're being a jackass.

ADAM. We're joking, babe. Lighten up.

LUKE. Is it so wrong of me to want you to go to heaven? I mean, what's the big fucking deal?

ADAM. Yes, because I don't believe in it, Luke. Not your version. It's too exclusive. Too many rules.

LUKE. Fine. Then I'll believe. For both of us. *(He continues unpacking.)*

ADAM. If you can believe so strongly, then how come you don't want me telling anyone you do?

LUKE. It's nobody's business! It's not something I go shouting from rooftops.

ADAM. You're embarrassed, Luke. Admit it.

LUKE. I just don't like being judged, Adam. And that's what everyone does. Before they even get a chance to know who I am, they all have this predisposed disdain.

ADAM. Who does?

LUKE. You do! You never would've even considered dating me if you knew when we first met.

ADAM. The only reason anyone judges you is because you go around judging everyone else. You guys are all about judgment. You even have a whole day named after it.

LUKE. I don't judge anyone. It's not my place to. I'm just here to tell you there's a heaven. Whether you listen or not, that's up to you.

ADAM. Oh, I'm listening, babe. Believe me. And if you and all the other freaks are going to be the only ones up there, then no thanks, I'd rather burn. *(Luke is speechless. He looks at Adam like he's a complete stranger all of a sudden, then gets up slowly and heads out the door.)*

HOLLY. Awkward.

ADAM. The afterlife. Can you believe that shit?

HOLLY. Like you don't have enough problems in this one.

ADAM. The stories these people have been fed, the antiquated bullshit. It's mind boggling. I swear, if I hear one more parable about a flock of fucking sheep. It's like Shakespeare. Why are we still doing him after all these years?

HOLLY. Yeah, what a hack. *(Adam sits on a box.)*

ADAM. Am I crazy? Does everyone think I'm nuts?

HOLLY. Not everyone.

ADAM. Martin and Bobby? Steven?

HOLLY. They do. Yes.

ADAM. Please, Steven's been dating abusive shits for years, and Martin and Bobby may as well be roommates.

HOLLY. They're just not sure what you're getting out of it, sweetie. Besides the fact that he's young and hot. Bobby thinks maybe it's just you, once again, falling for someone who's unavailable. And if it is, this time, he thinks you've hit the jackpot.

ADAM. Yeah, well, I think Bobby might wanna stop blowing his trainer if he's gonna throw stones from that glass house Martin pays for.

HOLLY. They're offended, Adam. Knowing how Luke feels. It's like an indictment of who they are.

ADAM. But he loves those guys!

HOLLY. Yeah, and he still thinks they're going to hell. It's self-loathing. And you're self-loathing by association.

ADAM. But it's all he knows. It's what kept the front door locked and the Pink Floyd off the stereo all these years.

HOLLY. Yeah, but at a certain point, you just have to break away from Mommy and Daddy and become your own person. I mean, I did. And my parents were big old Catholics.

ADAM. Not your dad.

HOLLY. Okay, but you can't get more Catholic than my mom. I mean, where did she take me for my sweet sixteen?

ADAM. The Vatican.

HOLLY. I'm just saying, there's a point when you just gotta wake up and smell the coffee. *(A beat.)*

ADAM. What about Belinda? What does she think?

HOLLY. There are lots of gays in her church, and none of them think they're sinners. She doesn't get it either.

ADAM. Yeah, well, I don't get why she named her kid Mustard Seed.

HOLLY. Saffron.

ADAM. Parsley, Tarragon, Bouillon Cube, whatever. It's weird.

HOLLY. I agree. She looks more like a root vegetable. *(Another beat.)*

ADAM. And you?

HOLLY. Me?

ADAM. Yeah. What do you think?

HOLLY. Truth?

ADAM. Yes, truth. No one calls me anymore.

HOLLY. What do you care what I think? Look within, sweetie. That's what my yoga teacher says.

ADAM. The one with the zero percent body fat?

HOLLY. He's a genius.

ADAM. Having a 29-inch waist and being able to breathe through your asshole does not a genius make. *(Holly sits down next to him.)*

HOLLY. Remember when you first started working at the shop? We'd hang out all the time. Couldn't get enough of each other. And at the end of the night, you'd walk me home. But only halfway. Maybe a block or two further, if I begged. But as soon as we hit 74th and Columbus, you'd turn around and leave me there. It used to piss me off. I don't know why. I just felt like you should've walked me all the way. But you'd only go so far. And that would make me want you to even more.

ADAM. Yeah. So?

HOLLY. Well, a few weeks ago, after that weird benefit for Katrina victims or, no, the kids with the club feet —

ADAM. — Cleft palates.

HOLLY. — Cleft palates, right. And you were walking me home, telling me that story about how Luke dropped a fan on your face in the middle of the night —

ADAM. — I had Honeywell branded on my forehead for over a —

HOLLY. — and there we were, suddenly, coming up to that same damn corner. I could just feel the dread rising in me. Old, stupid feelings, irrational ones, I know, but there they were again. Well, we hit 74th and you kept walking, past 75th and 76th, and before you know it, you'd walked me all the way to 82nd street, and you hadn't even noticed.

ADAM. I did? *(She looks at her watch.)*

HOLLY. Shit, I gotta run.

ADAM. You can't leave me like this.

HOLLY. I have to, sweetie. I'm late for my chanting group.

ADAM. Oh, Christ. What are you chanting for this week? A new boyfriend? A lot of good it's done you so far.

HOLLY. *(Stung.)* Thanks.

ADAM. I'm sorry. That was mean.

HOLLY. At least I'm trying. At least I'm open to it.

ADAM. I know. I'm a jerk.

HOLLY. You're always so good at figuring out exactly why something's not gonna work. This one's too this or that one's too that. These poor guys. It's like, they're all doomed from the get go.

ADAM. I'm usually right, though. I can't help it.

HOLLY. Did you ever think that maybe, in the end, you just don't have faith that any of them will stay? *(A beat.)*

ADAM. I'm still stuck on the whole walking-you-home analogy.

HOLLY. You're going places you've never been before, dummy. Who cares what the rest of us think. Let yourself go. *(She gives him a peck on the cheek and heads for the door, stopping before she exits.)* Are fag hags allowed in heaven? Not that I care or anything. Just curious.

ADAM. I don't see why not. No crime in being a fag hag.

HOLLY. Aiding and abetting?

ADAM. True. *(Holly goes, leaving Adam to take in the mess around him.)*

Scene 6

The waiting room. Butch flips through the Newsweek. *Arlene paces on her cell phone.*

ARLENE. Oh, for Pete's sake, how many did she eat? ... The whole box? ... Well, how the heck did that happen? Uh-huh ... Uh-huh ... Uh-huh ... *(She exits down the hallway as Adam enters with some vending machine candy. Butch tosses the* Newsweek *down.)*

BUTCH. Porn.

ADAM. *(Completely confused.)* What was that?

BUTCH. What was what?

ADAM. You said, "porn?"

BUTCH. Oh, I'm just goofing. *(Holly enters, in her coat.)*

HOLLY. You guys should really get outside for a bit. The air is gorgeous. *(She hangs it up.)*

HOLLY. They're still not letting anyone in?

ADAM. Nope.

BUTCH. How about a game of cards, Holly?

HOLLY. Me?

BUTCH. A little five-card stud?

HOLLY. I'm not really big on cards.

BUTCH. No?

HOLLY. I've got this weird competitive streak.

BUTCH. Is that right?

HOLLY. It isn't pretty.

BUTCH. Come on. I'll go easy on you.

HOLLY. I don't think so.

BUTCH. You sure?

HOLLY. Pretty sure.

BUTCH. Some gin rummy, maybe?

HOLLY. Don't tempt me.

BUTCH. Nickel a point. Jokers are wild.

HOLLY. Okay, you're on, mister.

BUTCH. 'Atta girl. *(Butch pulls out a deck of cards and starts shuffling. Holly takes a seat next to him.)*

HOLLY. I'm a little rusty, so let's take it slow.

BUTCH. Don't worry. I'll be gentle. We'll play the seven-card version. *(Adam picks up the* Newsweek *Butch just tossed down, and points to the prehistoric man on the cover.)*

ADAM. This guy, here?

BUTCH. What's that?

ADAM. The missing link?

BUTCH. Uh-huh?

ADAM. You find him pornographic?

BUTCH. I find it irresponsible, that's all.

ADAM. Funny, I look at him and I see my fifth-grade gym teacher.

BUTCH. Looks like an ape to me.

HOLLY. My fifth grade gym teacher was way hairier than that. Handsome woman. Looked just like a sheepdog. *(Holly and Butch pick up their cards.)*

BUTCH. Don't forget now, jokers are wild.

HOLLY. Got it.

ADAM. But don't apes and humans have a very similar genetic makeup?

BUTCH. I wouldn't know.

ADAM. We do. We're, like, one gene apart. I'm almost positive.

BUTCH. If you say so.

ADAM. You'd think there'd be some kind of correlation.

BUTCH. I'm feeling lucky, Holly.

ADAM. I mean, I'm not Einstein or anything. Just seems like a given.

BUTCH. Apes don't have souls, son. How can something without a soul morph into something with one? *(Arlene reenters, snapping her cell phone closed.)*

ARLENE. Well, Frieda shit all over the apartment.

HOLLY. Your housekeeper?

ARLENE. My dog. I don't have a housekeeper. That's Lynn,

remember? Butch's new and improved wife.

BUTCH. The one who doesn't talk so much.

ARLENE. No, I never had that luxury, did I, Butch? You were broke when we were married, weren't you, hon? *(She perches behind him and checks out his hand.)*

BUTCH. I told you not to get that damn dog. You can't take care of yourself, let alone a four-and-a-half-pound Chihuahua.

ARLENE. Oh, would you hush. The neighbor's got it all under control. She's gnawing on a bull penis, right now. The dog, not the … She'll be fine. She survived the streets of San Juan for eight months, she can crap on my carpet for another couple nights.

HOLLY. I'm sorry … bull penis?

ARLENE. They advertise it as beef tendon, but the Oriental lady at the pet store gave me the real skinny.

BUTCH. Sounds like what they served on the plane.

ARLENE. *(Re: cards.)* I wouldn't play that if I were you.

BUTCH. Do you mind?

ARLENE. Okay, buster, but don't say I didn't warn you. *(She scans the room for her purse.)*

ADAM. What about bats?

ARLENE. Bats?

ADAM. Rats with wings, right? There's gotta be some morphing going on there, don't you think?

BUTCH. We're back on that, are we?

ADAM. Or Siegfried and Roy? They morphed two species and came up with a liger. How do you explain that?

ARLENE. How do you explain Siegfried and Roy?

BUTCH. Must have been on the ark at the same time, that's how. I don't believe one morphed into the other.

HOLLY. Aces are low, right?

BUTCH. Yup.

ADAM. The ark? See, now, there's a concept I've never quite been able to wrap my head around.

ARLENE. Anyone seen my purse?

ADAM. All those animals on one little boat? I mean, does anyone else think that's a little over the top, or is it just me?

BUTCH. Says so right there in the Bible.

ADAM. I know, but the whole Bible sort of feels that way to me, with the parting of the seas and the walking on water.

HOLLY. Adam …

ADAM. I don't know. It all seems a little Vegas, for my taste.

BUTCH. I'm not the one who brought up Siegfried and Roy.

ARLENE. My purse, people. Who's got my … Oh. *(Arlene finds her purse and starts rooting through it.)*

ADAM. Might just be me though. I mean, I didn't grow up with the Bible, so I've never really had any sort of connection to it.

BUTCH. *(Re: cards.)* You're killing me, here.

ADAM. In fact, I could probably wipe myself with it today, and wake up tomorrow with a clean ass and a clear conscience. *(The game, the conversation, everything comes to a crashing halt.)*

ARLENE. I could have done without that visual.

ADAM. *(Backpedaling.)* Sorry. I was just trying to, you know, illustrate my point.

ARLENE. Oh no, hon, we got it.

ADAM. I'm just saying. Give me an argument that means something. Give me science.

BUTCH. Science isn't all it's cracked up to be, son. They told us the world was flat for centuries. Sometimes it's just a tool used to disprove the word of God. Says so in the Bible. If you weren't so busy wiping your ass with it, maybe you'd know that. *(The two men stare at each other. Holly lays her cards down, awkwardly.)*

HOLLY. Gin. *(Butch throws his cards in.)*

BUTCH. Beginner's luck. Double or nothing. *(Arlene gently tries to tug her coat out from underneath him.)*

BUTCH. Would you knock it off?

ARLENE. You're on my coat, Butch. *(He grabs hold of it.)*

BUTCH. What do you need it for?

ARLENE. What do you mean, what do I need it for? I'm cold.

BUTCH. Don't snow me, Arlene.

ARLENE. I'm not snowing you.

BUTCH. Bullcrap.

ARLENE. Nobody's snowing anybody, Butch. Let go.

BUTCH. You want me to let go?

ARLENE. I mean it.

BUTCH. Oh, I know you do.

ARLENE. Butch! *(Butch lets the coat go. Arlene falls backward, and lands on her ass. It's a startling moment. Adam and Holly aren't quite sure what to do as Butch pulls her bottle of pills out and holds them in the air.)*

BUTCH. Is this what you were looking for? *(He tosses them at her.)*

It took you five years to get off that crap, and five hours to get back on it.

ARLENE. Butch …

BUTCH. Don't "Butch" me. Our son's in a coma, sweetheart. Start dealing with it. *(Butch storms out of the room. Adam and Holly look at each other uncomfortably as Arlene slowly picks herself up off the floor.)*

ARLENE. *(Trying to recover.)* Boy, oh, boy. That was like *Jerry Springer* time, wasn't it? *(She pockets the pills and hangs her coat back up.)* Don't mind him. He's just … upset, is all. *(She straightens her skirt.)* Better go see if I can … calm him down. *(Brandon enters, a concerned look on his face.)* Brandon?

BRANDON. It's Luke … They need you in there. *(Arlene holds her hand to her heart, then rushes offstage.)*

HOLLY. What's going on, Brandon?

BRANDON. I'm not sure … He's … Something's changed. *(Holly looks to Adam helplessly as the lights fade.)*

End of Act One

ACT TWO

Scene 1

The waiting room. Brandon sits alone. Holly enters, in a daze.

BRANDON. How's everyone holding up in there?

HOLLY. I don't know. Okay, I guess. You going back in?

BRANDON. I think I'll stay out here for a while.

HOLLY. Me, too. *(Holly puts on a sweater.)*

BRANDON. Has Adam talked to them yet?

HOLLY. There hasn't exactly been a good time. He spoke to the surgeon though.

BRANDON. And?

HOLLY. He thinks Adam should do whatever he can to persuade Butch and Arlene to, you know, do "the right thing." How do you make that call?

BRANDON. Yeah.

HOLLY. There's an organ-transplant representative lurking around, smiling at everyone. Which is creepy. *(A beat.)* Would that be considered murder in their eyes, Brandon? I mean, what's the general consensus?

BRANDON. It's different for everyone. Butch and Arlene? Who knows where they stand?

HOLLY. Yeah, well, I know where I stand. Life's grand and all, but no thank you. *(Another beat.)* At least, I think that's where I stand. I mean, it's one thing to say it, but to actually have to ... The whole thing is so confusing, all of a sudden.

BRANDON. Yeah. *(Holly notices Brandon's empty-handed.)*

HOLLY. Do you mind if I take a look at your ... uh ... Never mind ...

BRANDON. Bible? *(She nods, sheepishly.)* Arlene has it.

HOLLY. It's funny ... Moments like this ... How ingrained this stuff becomes ... I mean, I sell candles for a living. I've been to fucking ashrams and silent meditation retreats. I've got like five

42

yoga mats in my closet … But I haven't stopped crossing myself since I got here. *(They sit in silence.)*
HOLLY. What about you, Brandon?
BRANDON. Me?
HOLLY. Yeah, where do you stand?
BRANDON. I think I probably feel the same way Adam does.
HOLLY. Really?
BRANDON. But for different reasons.
HOLLY. How so?
BRANDON. When it's your time, it's your time. That's what I believe. There's a plan for Luke. A perfect one. And I don't believe in getting in the way of that.
HOLLY. I guess.
BRANDON. But it's not really for me to say. *(Holly thinks about this for a moment, then …)*
HOLLY. Do you think it's for Adam to say?

Scene 2

Adam and Luke's apartment. Three years earlier. Adam enters through the front door, and turns off the Christian rock that Luke's got blaring.

LUKE. *(Offstage.)* Babe?
ADAM. Hi.
LUKE. *(Offstage.)* What are you doing home?
ADAM. My leg's bothering me. I hope I'm not getting a clot or something.
LUKE. *(Offstage.)* A clot?
ADAM. Yeah, like what that cute reporter in Iraq died from?
LUKE. *(Offstage.)* Thrombosis.
ADAM. He had a wife and kids and everything, poor guy.
LUKE. *(Offstage.)* You don't have a thrombosis, Adam.
ADAM. I hope not. *(Adam opens the closet door and a bunch of crap falls out. Unphased, he hangs his coat up, stuffs the crap back in, and heads for the kitchen.)* I'm making tea. Want some? *(Luke rushes in*

from the bedroom.)

LUKE. Will you help me get rid of this thing in the bedroom?

ADAM. *(Offstage.)* What thing?

LUKE. The ass photo.

ADAM. *(Offstage.)* My Mapplethorpe knockoff? It cost me a fortune. Why would I wanna get rid of it?

LUKE. Never mind. *(On a mission, Luke starts plucking books off the bookshelf. Adam reenters, with his pants rolled up.)*

ADAM. Does my left calf look bigger than my right?

LUKE. *(Not looking.)* No.

ADAM. It feels bigger. *(Adam sits, examining his calf.)*

LUKE. How long does it take to get here from JFK?

ADAM. I don't know. Forty-five minutes, depending on traffic. Why?

LUKE. My dad just called.

ADAM. So?

LUKE. From JFK. He's on his way over. *(Luke grabs the books and makes a beeline for the closet.)*

ADAM. Wait a minute. What?

LUKE. Hasn't thought about New York in thirty years and all of a sudden he's nostalgic.

ADAM. You mean I finally get to meet him?

LUKE. Not if I can help it. *(Luke opens the closet door and the crap falls out again.)* Would you mind giving me a hand here? We don't have much time.

ADAM. To what?

LUKE. De-gay the apartment. *(Luke shoves all the crap back in, heads into the bedroom.)*

ADAM. *(Panicked.)* Your father's coming?

LUKE. *(Offstage.)* Like any minute.

ADAM. What's he in town for?

LUKE. Some auction. I don't know. The whole thing was very last minute. Very spontaneous. Very, you know, psychotic. *(Luke reenters with a Tinky Winky doll and tosses it into the closet.)* He wants to check out my apartment while he's here.

ADAM. Our apartment.

LUKE. Yeah, well he doesn't know that. Are you gonna help me with the ass photo or what?

ADAM. I like that ass photo. It took me three years to pay for it.

LUKE. Well, I don't want it hanging over the bed when he gets here.

ADAM. How about I hang you over the bed?

LUKE. Is that a Capote book on the top shelf? *(Luke snatches it off the bookshelf and tosses it onto the couch.)*

ADAM. Why don't you grow some hair on your balls and just tell him already?

LUKE. *(Offstage.)* Are you nuts? I told you what he said when I quit law school.

ADAM. No, you didn't.

LUKE. *(Offstage.)* He said he'd never let me speak to my little brother again if he ever found out I was gay.

ADAM. And you don't think he knows?! All those years you were doing splits in your backyard in your little Richard Simmons shorts? Just tell him, already.

LUKE. *(Offstage.)* I will. I promise. *(Luke reenters with an armful of framed photos, and heads for the bookshelf.)* Next fall. When Ben's in college. I figure by then he'll be old enough to decide for himself.

ADAM. Now what?

LUKE. Photos.

ADAM. Luke!

LUKE. Just the lovey-dovey ones … I'm gonna put a few of my old ones up, just to, you know, sell the place a little more. *(He takes some photos off the bookshelf, and replaces them with new ones. Adam grabs one and looks at it.)*

ADAM. Who's that?

LUKE. My little brother.

ADAM. Looks like Adolf Hitler as a young girl. *(Luke snatches it back, cleaning it with his shirt sleeve.)*

LUKE. I can't believe how filthy these got.

ADAM. You know, one of these days, it's all gonna come crashing down on you.

LUKE. Yeah, like today, if you don't start giving me a hand.

ADAM. And I ain't gonna be around to pick up the pieces.

LUKE. Windex. We need Windex. Would you mind running down to the deli?

ADAM. Absolutely not.

LUKE. Adam?!

ADAM. No, Luke. I refuse to participate in this homophobic bullshit.

LUKE. Then would you please start thinking of someplace to go, because I can't have you around when he gets here. *(Luke selects a few photos, picks the box up and stands. The bottom of the box breaks, sending the photos everywhere.)*

LUKE. Fuck! *(He gets on his hands and knees, desperately trying to collect them all.)* This would be so much easier if you'd just give me a fucking hand.

ADAM. Look at you.

LUKE. What, Adam? What?!

ADAM. You're like an animal in a trap trying to gnaw your own leg off. *(This hits Luke for a moment, but then he quickly springs back into action.)*

LUKE. Fine. I'll get it myself. *(He leaves the mess on the floor and bolts for the front door.)* But I want you out of here when I get back. I'm serious. Just for an hour or two. *(Pleading.)* Please. *(He exits, leaving the door slightly ajar. Adam crosses over and yells after him.)*

ADAM. I ain't going anywhere, sweet tits. You'll have to stuff me in the closet with the rest of the incriminating evidence. *(He looks at the photos on the floor.)* Lovey-dovey ones? *(He picks one up.)* I didn't even like you on this vacation. *(He tosses it back into the box. Picks up another, and tosses it in. And before you know it, he's cleaned up the entire mess.)* Crazy. *(Grabbing the Capote book and placing it defiantly back up on the shelf, he picks up the box, and exits into the bedroom. There's a knock at the door.)*

BUTCH. *(Offstage.)* Hello? *(Butch pokes his head in, then enters, tentatively.)*

ADAM. *(Offstage.)* I can't believe you took this thing down. What, the man's never seen a big black ass before? *(Adam comes out of the bedroom, the ass photo in his arms. He stops short when he sees Butch standing there.)*

BUTCH. I'm sorry. I must have the wrong apartment.

ADAM. No ... um ... He's ... He went to the deli.

BUTCH. I see.

ADAM. For Windex.

BUTCH. Okay.

ADAM. He should be back any second.

BUTCH. Terrific. *(They stand there for a minute.)*

ADAM. Excuse me, for a minute. *(Adam exits back into the bedroom with the photo. Butch takes the place in. He hears a loud crash. Offstage.)* Shit. *(Adam returns, flustered.)*

BUTCH. Everything okay in there?

ADAM. It's fine. *(They stand there, awkwardly.)*

BUTCH. I'm Luke's dad.

ADAM. From Florida.

BUTCH. Tallahassee, right.

ADAM. You're in for an auction?

BUTCH. I am.

ADAM. Cool. *(Adam's teakettle whistles.)* My water's boiling.

BUTCH. Do what you gotta do. *(Adam starts off, then turns.)*

ADAM. Would you like some?

BUTCH. Some?

ADAM. Tea?

BUTCH. Sure. What the heck. *(Adam exits into the kitchen. Butch checks out the pad.)* Swanky place.

ADAM. *(Offstage.)* Yeah, it's … you know … serviceable.

BUTCH. How long's he been living here?

ADAM. *(Offstage.)* Who?

BUTCH. Luke.

ADAM. *(Offstage.)* Oh … Um … two years, I guess?

BUTCH. Two, really? How about that? *(He wanders over to the window and stares out. Adam reenters with two cups of tea.)*

ADAM. Here you go.

BUTCH. They're gone.

ADAM. Excuse me?

BUTCH. The towers. You can't help but notice on the way in from the airport.

ADAM. Oh, yeah. If you look down to your right there, you can see where they were.

BUTCH. I spent a semester here in college. The year they started construction on them. I used to go down, once or twice a month, to check out the progress. Watch them work their way into the sky. Made me feel proud to be here. New York. Like I was part of something.

ADAM. Honey? *(Adam holds up a honey bear.)*

BUTCH. Straight's fine. *(He hands Butch his tea.)* Nice cups. *(They blow on their tea.)* Dainty.

ADAM. So, you spent a semester here?

BUTCH. Working for Carl Randolph, yeah. They're auctioning off his entire estate this afternoon.

ADAM. You're going to the Carl Randolph auction?

BUTCH. Uh-huh.

ADAM. At Sotheby's?

BUTCH. He was sort of a mentor to me.

ADAM. That's, like, the hottest ticket in town.

BUTCH. I've got my eye on a set of books. *Hardy Boys.* First editions. Fifteen, maybe twenty volumes. All signed and in pristine condition. He kept them on display in his office. As a reminder, I guess. Of his childhood. His youthful aspirations. That always sort of stuck with me, and I thought I might like to have them.

ADAM. Carl Randolph? God, he was, like, huge in the eighties. He made Donald Trump look like, well, Donald Trump. I used to see him on the subway, once in a while. No entourage. No bodyguards. Just him. And I thought that was so cool. I mean, there he was, acting like he was one of us, when really he was, you know, Carl Randolph. *(Butch smiles.)*

BUTCH. And who are you?

ADAM. Who am I? *(That hangs in the air for a second, until Luke enters, instantly thrown when he sees Butch standing there.)*

LUKE. Dad!

BUTCH. Hello, son.

LUKE. That was quick.

BUTCH. Saheed was a yakker with a lead foot.

LUKE. And … so … you're having tea? *(He sets the Windex down and quickly cases the joint.)*

BUTCH. Your friend here made it.

LUKE. Then you two have met?

BUTCH. We were just getting to that.

LUKE. This is Adam, Dad. We work together.

BUTCH. At the flower shop?

ADAM/LUKE. Candles.

LUKE. Adam's been there longer than I have.

ADAM. Too long. I'm trying to move on.

LUKE. For two years he's been saying that.

ADAM. Not two. Besides, I had a teaching interview today, and —

BUTCH. So, this is it, huh, kiddo? *(Butch meanders around the place.)*

LUKE. This is what?

BUTCH. Your bachelor pad. *(Luke avoids Adam's look.)*

LUKE. Yup. This is it.

BUTCH. How about that? *(Luke spots the Capote book, nabs it off the shelf, glaring at Adam as he heads into the bedroom.)*

LUKE. So, how was your flight?

BUTCH. Easy. Quick. Your mom thinks I've lost it.

LUKE. Well, it is a little out of the blue, Dad.

BUTCH. I know, but what the heck. Life's short and then you die. *(A beat.)*

ADAM. And then what happens? *(Butch turns from the bookshelf. Adam smiles, innocently.)*

LUKE. *(Offstage.)* Oh, no! What happened to the ass pho ... the Mapplethorpe knockoff.

ADAM. I broke it.

LUKE. *(Offstage.)* Babe! *(Adam blanches at Luke's faux pas. Luke reenters, white as a sheet. Butch turns from the bookshelf. He's hard to read.)*

BUTCH. Where's the bathroom?

LUKE. In there.

BUTCH. Excuse me, men. *(Luke watches, mortified, as his dad exits into the bathroom.)*

LUKE. I can't believe I just said that.

ADAM. I don't think he heard.

LUKE. Are you crazy? Of course, he heard.

ADAM. And, so what if he did?

LUKE. This is unbelievable.

ADAM. Come on, babe. He knows. He called our cups "dainty."

LUKE. Well, they are dainty.

ADAM. He thinks you work at a flower shop. He likes the *Hardy Boys.* He knows. He knows.

LUKE. Somebody shoot me.

ADAM. He worked for Carl Randolph, Luke. The guy was his mentor.

LUKE. So?

ADAM. So? Carl Randolph was gay.

LUKE. No, he wasn't. He had a wife and kids.

ADAM. He was a big old leather queen. They wrote about it in *Vanity Fair* last month.

LUKE. Oh, my God.

ADAM. Just tell him, already. I'll tell him with you. We'll hold hands and walk into the fire together.

LUKE. Or I could pretend the whole thing never happened. I'm good at that.

ADAM. Come on, Luke. You don't want to end up like one of those people.

LUKE. What people?

ADAM. Who wake up in the middle of the night ... Screaming. *(They hear the toilet flush.)*

LUKE. Okay, but if I'm gonna walk into the fire, I'm gonna do it alone. Just me and him. *Mano a mano.*

ADAM. You want me to go?

LUKE. Yes. Please. Quick. Before I change my mind.

ADAM. I'm so proud of you. *(They go to kiss, but quickly think the better of it.)* I'll be on my cell if you need me. *(Adam scoots out the door. Luke takes a deep breath as Butch reenters from the bathroom.)*

BUTCH. Tight squeeze in there.

LUKE. Yeah … you know … New York.

BUTCH. I like how you've got all those pictures on the wall. Gives you something to look at while you're on the crapper.

LUKE. *(Bracing himself.)* Dad? *(Butch hands over a framed photo.)*

BUTCH. This one must have fallen.

LUKE. Oh, thanks.

BUTCH. These are the folks you did that Huck Finn play with, right?

LUKE. Yeah.

BUTCH. You were good in that. *(Pause.)* You all were.

LUKE. Really?

BUTCH. Well, most of you … I mean, I'm no patron of the arts, but … this play … that was … something.

LUKE. Are you kidding me?

BUTCH. Am I wrong?

LUKE. No, it's just … I'm just a little shocked, that's all.

BUTCH. Listen, I know I'm not the most supportive parent in the world. I thought it was a big mistake when you left law school, I'm not gonna lie to you. But that play … I don't know, I guess I kinda started to see how the acting thing might be something you could be proud of someday.

LUKE. Wow …

BUTCH. I mean, money isn't everything, right?

LUKE. Totally. I love it. *(Butch sits with his tea. Luke joins him, forgetting, for a moment, the task at hand.)*

BUTCH. I remember some jerk was sitting in front of me. Yakkin' the whole time, buggin' everyone, so I start shushing him, telling him to be quiet, and he turns around, like, what's your problem, and I say, "That's my son up there, and if you don't start paying attention, I'm gonna bop you one." And boy, if that didn't shut him up. *(The two men share a laugh, connecting finally, like old pals. Luke feels comfortable enough to continue.)*

LUKE. Listen, Dad …

BUTCH. Let me ask you something though, kiddo. And this is something I was always curious about.

LUKE. Sure.

BUTCH. *(Curious.)* Was the nigger a fag?

LUKE. Excuse me?

BUTCH. This guy here. The one who played the slave. He was a fag, right? *(Butch points to the photo.)* He was kinda swishy, that's all. Like I said, I don't know my ass from my elbow when it comes to this acting stuff, I just thought it would have been nice to have someone a little more …

LUKE. White?

BUTCH. Manly … in the part. *(Butch gives him a wink.)* But what the heck do I know? *(He rises.)* So, where'd your friend go?

LUKE. *(Completely stunned.)* Oh, his leg hurt. Thrombosis or something.

BUTCH. Thrombosis?

LUKE. I don't know. There's always something going on with him.

BUTCH. Okay, well, come on then. Let's eat. *(Butch makes his way to the door. Luke just sits there, completely sucker-punched.)*

Scene 3

Adam's apartment. A year later. Adam, in his underwear, sits in front of his laptop, the glow of the screen illuminating his face.

LUKE. *(Offstage.)* Adam?

ADAM. *(Busted.)* Yeah?

LUKE. *(Offstage.)* What are you doing?

ADAM. Nothing. Go back to sleep. *(Adam goes back to the screen.)*

LUKE. *(Offstage.)* Are you on that website again? *(Adam looks up again, guilty.)*

ADAM. What website?

LUKE. *(Offstage.)* The brain tumor website. *(Adam quickly snaps the laptop shut, as Luke enters from the bedroom, half asleep.)* You promised.

ADAM. I know I did. *(He joins Adam on the couch.)*

LUKE. Tell me what the doctor said again.

ADAM. *(Obsessed.)* It could be a sinus infection, some kind of vertigo thing, a virus … He doesn't know.

LUKE. He said it wasn't a brain tumor, Adam.

ADAM. He said he didn't *think* it was a brain tumor. He can't say for sure.

LUKE. You're still feeling dizzy?

ADAM. Not dizzy … Fuzzy. Like my brain is swollen or something.

LUKE. What about the headache?

ADAM. It's more like my hair aches. Like my follicles are sore. *(Luke stares at Adam, blankly.)* And now the squishy noise is back.

LUKE. Okay, you need therapy.

ADAM. It got so distracting I had to cancel my AP English class this afternoon.

LUKE. Please, don't sabotage this teaching stuff, Adam. It took you so long to finally make the change.

ADAM. I can't help it! The fuzziness. The ringing. It's not normal.

LUKE. You're telling me?

ADAM. I'm serious! *(Adam gets up and starts pacing. Luke sees that he's really spiraling this time.)*

LUKE. Why don't you go get an MRI then? Come on, babe, I'll go with you. So we can know it's not a brain tumor, once and for all, and relax.

ADAM. But what if it is?

LUKE. You have to stop, Adam. Seriously. When there are so many people who really do have something to worry about?

ADAM. I know.

LUKE. You have so much to be thankful for.

ADAM. I know. I know.

LUKE. Then why do you keep trying to fuck it all up?

ADAM. It's not like I'm trying. It's not like I'm thinking, "Huh, life's pretty good right now. Maybe I should give myself a brain tumor."

LUKE. You're unhappy, babe.

ADAM. I know I'm unhappy. My fucking head hurts! You'd be unhappy, too!

LUKE. In life … It's like you don't feel you deserve to be, or something. Like the minute you actually do, it's all gonna be taken away from you. I mean, what are you so afraid of? *(A beat.)*

ADAM. Oh, God. We're gonna go there, aren't we?

LUKE. Where?

ADAM. To Jesus land. Go ahead. I know you want to.

LUKE. I didn't say anything.

ADAM. *(Helpless.)* Why is it every time I reach out to you, every time there's some kind of crisis in my life, this is the only thing you have to offer?

LUKE. What are you talking about?

ADAM. It is, Luke.

LUKE. I don't know what you're talking about, Adam.

ADAM. Like when my dad died.

LUKE. I was there for you.

ADAM. Come on.

LUKE. I was fucking there for you, Adam! I flew halfway across the country to be there for you. I held his ashes in my lap on the way home from the service. I mean, what more do you want?

ADAM. That's not what I'm talking about.

LUKE. I sat in a different pew because you didn't want anyone to feel "uncomfortable." I took communion while you and the rest of your family just sat there like idiots. I practically wrote his whole fucking eulogy for you. Don't tell me I wasn't there, Adam. I was there.

ADAM. Before, Luke. I'm talking about the night he died. We were lying in bed together. And you looked at me, all of a sudden, with this, it was almost smug, Luke. This holier than-thou look of pity on your face —

LUKE. — I was trying to comfort you!

ADAM. It didn't mean anything! Don't you get it? You may as well have been speaking a foreign fucking language! And for that to be the only thing you have to offer, at a time when I needed you the most. I'm sorry, but I've never felt so alone in all my life.

LUKE. Well, what did you want me to do?

ADAM. Hold me! *(A beat.)* I just wanted you to fucking hold me, Luke! Is that so hard to understand? *(Another beat.)*

LUKE. A little.

ADAM. Forget it.

LUKE. I'm sorry, but it is.

ADAM. I don't even know why I bothered to bring it up.

LUKE. Because I'm not afraid like you are, Adam. When the time comes ... I welcome it. *(Gentle.)* You could, too.

ADAM. You're doing it again.

LUKE. I just hate to see you in pain like this.

ADAM. Listen, I would love that, believe me … It's like the one thing I envy you for … To know everything's gonna be alright … No matter what … To feel … safe like that? It would almost be worth it.

LUKE. It is worth it, Adam. It's so worth it.

ADAM. But I've never had that in my life, so how would I know for sure? I wasn't the one sitting in my dad's Chrysler LeBaron when the white light —

LUKE. — It wasn't a white light.

ADAM. The warmth, the peace, whatever it was —

LUKE. Home, Adam. *(A pause.)* I felt home. For the first time in my life … It's there, babe. You just have to be open to it. *(Adam, sits, completely lost.)*

ADAM. This all started back in college. I had mono and thought for sure it was AIDS. It was before there was even a test, remember?

LUKE. I was eight.

ADAM. Well, it was horrible, trust me. And I remember being convinced, at the time, that it was, like my punishment.

LUKE. Punishment?

ADAM. For being gay.

LUKE. Punishment from whom?

ADAM. Oh, I don't know … God, I guess. *(A beat.)* You don't have to believe in hell to walk around feeling like you're gonna burn in it. *(Another beat.)*

LUKE. What if He wasn't a punisher? *(Luke moves closer.)* You mentioned your soul the night we first met.

ADAM. I did?

LUKE. You said it was fat. That's how I knew we were meant to be. *(He wraps his arms around Adam.)* You believe, Adam. I know you do … And I knew that night on the rooftop … whether you had or you hadn't yet … I knew that one day you'd see. *(Adam closes his eyes.)* Please, Adam … For me. *(He sits there, open for something to happen. Nothing. So, he squeezes them tighter, desperately trying to feel the warmth, something. Still nothing. He gives it one last shot, his face softening this time, and there's a peace that washes over him. A calm. Then, after what seems like an eternity, Adam opens his eyes again, and finds himself back where he started.)*

ADAM. I'm gonna get a sleeping pill. *(He gets up and heads for*

the bathroom.)
LUKE. *(Crestfallen.)* Make it two.
ADAM. Can we wear our new sleeping masks?
LUKE. Sure ... As long as it doesn't, you know, make your hair hurt. *(Luke opens the laptop and stares at Adam's madness on the screen.)* Remember that huge fight we had a few years back?
ADAM. *(Offstage.)* About the rapture?
LUKE. And I said that thing about the cancer patient, and the pill and all that? *(Adam reenters and hands over a sleeping pill.)*
ADAM. Vaguely. *(Luke holds the pill up for Adam to see, then pops it in his mouth and swallows.)*
LUKE. See? *(Adam considers this for a moment.)*
ADAM. Yeah, but come on, babe. If it were that easy, who wouldn't swallow it? *(He picks up his laptop and exits, leaving Luke there in limbo.)*

Scene 4

A small makeshift temple in Beth Israel. Arlene sits quietly, Brandon's Bible in her lap. Adam enters, tentatively. Arlene scoots over to make room. He braces himself and joins her.

ARLENE. Quiet, isn't it?
ADAM. Yeah ... *(They take the place in. Torahs. A huge Star of David. Prayer shawls. A bowl of yarmulkes, maybe.)*
ARLENE. They have this elevator here, some nice lady was telling me, it automatically stops on every floor. And I thought, now what on earth would you want that for? Turns out they're not supposed to use electricity on weekends. Jewish people. It's against their religion.
ADAM. I think it was about energy, originally. You weren't supposed to exert any on the Sabbath. Sort of like an "And on the seventh day He rested" kind of thing. But then, I guess, as time went on and technology advanced, it included all the new and improved gadgets that made life easier.
ARLENE. I see ... Well, I guess they're allowed to use all of that now, they're just not allowed to push any buttons. *(She stares some*

more at her surroundings.) So many things to consider.

ADAM. I'm sure.

ARLENE. And never having been in this position before.

ADAM. Of course.

ARLENE. Just need a little more time to …

ADAM. Sort things out?

ARLENE. Pray. *(Adam notices the Bible in her lap.)* I'm one, too. Does that surprise you?

ADAM. Me? No. I'm … No, not at all.

ARLENE. At least I think I am. Who knows anymore. But then I grab hold of this thing. So familiar. Like an old friend. I read a passage I've read a thousand times before … It gives me comfort somehow. Butch is a whole other story. He really clings to the damn thing for dear life, poor guy … I'm sure that's my fault, too. Just another victim of Lung Lady's evil ways.

ADAM. Lung Lady?

ARLENE. Oh, that's just something I started calling myself after we split.

ADAM. Were you a big smoker?

ARLENE. No. Well, yes. I was. But that's not why. *(A beat.)* I used to be a bit of a loose cannon. We both were. Butch and me. Couple of crazies. But at a certain point, Butch had enough, pulled himself together, and I just sank further into it all. I'd disappear for days at a time. Weeks even. Then six months in jail. For selling pot. Not even selling, really. Oh, it's a long stupid story, involving my ex-best friend, a one-armed beautician from Shreveport, I kid you not, but I was just a fool. Mad at the world and no one was gonna tell me otherwise. Not even this sweet little kid. When I got out, I was so determined to make it up to him, I scraped together some cash and bought him a bicycle. It had the sparkly tassels, the wicker basket, and everything just like he wanted, and he wouldn't look at the damn thing. Just sat in his sandbox, ignoring me. So, I started stomping my foot and screaming at the little shit. "Now, you listen to me, young man." Like, all of a sudden, I'm gonna be a mother, right? Well, Luke's not having it, and he shouts back, "No, you listen to me, lung lady." And we just glare at each other for a minute, like a couple of mules, then I fell out laughing, and I thought, you know, he's right. That's what I've become. One of those evil cartoon characters. Flames bursting out my metallic bustier … With dark and mysterious powers no one would ever understand.

ADAM. Lung Lady.

ARLENE. Of course, that's not what he meant, but the name sorta stuck. Eventually, I worked my way into the sandbox with him. He's sitting there all angry and defiant, just like his mama. And all of a sudden I can't speak. Afraid I might break him. Or lose him. He wiggles his little toes up against mine and asks if people can glue their feet together. And I say, "Well, now, why would anyone wanna do that?" And he looks up at me with those big, blue eyes and says, "So no one can ever separate us." *(It all comes flooding back to her.)* Well, that just took my breath away. And I realized I had to leave again … So, Lung Lady crawled back into her hole for another ten years until she was ready to resurface. Butch met Lynn not long after, so Luke finally had some … stability. Of course, who can recognize her now, with all the work she's had done, but she's a good mom. Gave him a little brother who adores him. And me … *(Arlene takes out a Kleenex and blows her nose.)* Better see how Butch is doing. *(She rises.)*

ADAM. Um …

ARLENE. Yes?

ADAM. Luke and I … We're … *(Adam rises, not quite sure how to proceed.)* He means so much to me … *(A beat.)* All of us, really … But especially … *(Another beat.)* He's always loved his life … Just as it is, you know? And now … Well, I can't imagine he'd be happy any other way … He just wouldn't … I know it.

ARLENE. I suppose you're right. *(They stare at each other for a moment.)* You know, I got a chance to speak to the EMT guy when we first got here. A young black man. Very nice. Apparently, Luke went into shock right away, so there wasn't any pain, thank God.

ADAM. Yes.

ARLENE. But he kept asking for someone, just before he lost consciousness. It was faint, apparently, a little difficult to decipher, but the name, it sounded a lot like yours. *(Brandon enters.)*

BRANDON. Your husband is asking for you.

ARLENE. Thank you, Brandon. *(Arlene gives Adam's hand a squeeze.)* I'll see what I can do. *(She hands Brandon his Bible, and turns to Adam one last time.)* Butch wasn't with me when the EMT guy told me all that, and I don't think I'll mention it to him. He's a good man, Butch, but he's not perfect. *(She exits, leaving Adam and Brandon alone for the first time.)*

BRANDON. They're getting a hotel room.

ADAM. Oh, yeah?

BRANDON. Butch says he'll think better if he lays down for a few hours.

ADAM. Probably a good idea. *(A beat.)*

BRANDON. Adam …

ADAM. You were his emergency contact.

BRANDON. His …

ADAM. In his cell phone … You were the first one they called.

BRANDON. *(Embarassed, almost.)* Oh … Yeah.

ADAM. *(Searching.)* I always thought he would change that, but … I guess …

BRANDON. Might be a good time for you to be alone with him. I'll keep an eye out, you know. Just in case.

ADAM. *(Wary.)* Why are you doing this?

BRANDON. Don't ask why, Adam. Just go … Go. *(Adam looks at him for a moment longer, then exits. Brandon takes the place in. He picks a yarmulke out of the bowl and stares at it.)*

Scene 5

Central Park. A year ago. Adam waits near a bench. Brandon joins him with two cups of coffee.

ADAM. Is this okay?

BRANDON. Sure. *(He hands one over.)*

ADAM. This is, like, the fourth cup I've had today. What do I owe you?

BRANDON. Please. It's on me.

ADAM. Thanks. *(They sit.)* So … Long time, huh?

BRANDON. It has been.

ADAM. I read that article in the *Times* a few weeks ago. About the big merger. Congratulations.

BRANDON. Thanks. Things are … I just got promoted, too, so …

ADAM. Fantastic! Should've gotten a Venti.

BRANDON. And you?

ADAM. I left the candle shop a while back. I think you knew that.

BRANDON. I think I did, yeah.

ADAM. It was time, you know?

BRANDON. Are you liking it? Teaching?

ADAM. Sure. You know, you get the summer off. The kids are great. It's all good.

BRANDON. Good. *(Awkward smiles.)* Hey listen, do you want your rug back?

ADAM. My rug?

BRANDON. The purple one with the frayed edges?

ADAM. Oh, God. No. Please. ... We don't have room for it. Consider it permanently on loan ... For now.

BRANDON. Well, anytime you want it.

ADAM. I don't even like that rug.

BRANDON. Okay. *(More awkward smiling.)* How's Luke?

ADAM. Good. He's ... That's actually why I called.

BRANDON. I figured.

ADAM. Right? I mean, it's not like we, you and I, it's not like we ever ...

BRANDON. Yeah ...

ADAM. And I feel bad about that. I do. I mean, I always hoped we'd be friends, but that never quite happened, did it?

BRANDON. Not really. No.

ADAM. And I never understood why. Or why you and Luke stopped hanging out, for that matter. I have an idea. I mean, we've all been in that position before, right?

BRANDON. What position is that?

ADAM. Oh, you know, having a friendship, a close friendship. Maybe there's an unrequited thing, maybe not. I don't know. Whatever. Then someone else enters the dynamic and fucks it all up.

BRANDON. Uh-huh.

ADAM. It's painful to be around. I get it. I'd do the same thing.

BRANDON. Would you?

ADAM. But it's been like three years, Brandon.

BRANDON. Adam ...

ADAM. I'm sorry.

BRANDON. It's just kind of between Luke and me.

ADAM. No, you're right. *(A beat.)* Then, I guess, you coming for Thanksgiving, I guess, that's not gonna ...

BRANDON. I don't think so.

ADAM. It would mean so much to him. He's deep frying a

turkey. He's making sweet potatoes and collard greens, and all this Southern shit.

BRANDON. Um ...

ADAM. Never mind. *(Another beat.)*

BRANDON. So is that all you wanted to talk about?

ADAM. I guess so ... Yeah.

BRANDON. Because I've got an appointment I've got to —

ADAM. Actually, there is something else ... Do you have a second?

BRANDON. Sure.

ADAM. God, this is awkward ... Is it okay if I just sort of dive in here? Okay ... So, Luke and I have been together a little over four years now —

BRANDON. Four? Wow!

ADAM. I know, who would have thunk it, right? And things are great, all things considered. More than great, really. I mean, we've got our issues, but who doesn't, right? Like, he's still not out to his parents, which is just sort of boring at this point, but frankly, they don't seem like the kind of folks I really want to spend a holiday with, so ... Plus, he's out everywhere else in life, so it's mostly normal. It's a negotiation, like any relationship. He lets me watch CNN 24/7, I let him watch that show where people hop across the big, rubber balls and fall into the mud. He puts up with my tirades about the health care reform, I put up with his Martha Stewart magazines all over the place. He drops a fan on my face in the middle of the night, I —

BRANDON. Got it, Adam.

ADAM. We make compromises, that's all I'm saying. He's not even that extreme as far as all the Jesus stuff goes. He's pro choice. He believes in stem cell research. I think he might even vote for a Democrat in the next election.

BRANDON. Someone you can bring home to mom, I get it.

ADAM. And I have. Many times. And she loves him. Oh, and we're talking about having a baby now, too. Well, I'm talking, but he's nodding his head a lot. So, it's mostly good.

BRANDON. Great. So, what's the problem?

ADAM. The praying after sex. *(A beat.)* That's the one little quirk I'm still having a hard time with. *(Another beat.)* I know we've never talked about this kind of thing before, you and I. I mean, I don't even know if you're openly gay ... Or unopenly gay, even. I assume you're gay ... Or gayish. Gay friendly, at least. So, if you are ... and you do ... I mean, is that something you do, too? Pray after sex?

(Brandon's speechless.) You don't have to answer. I'm sorry. It's just something that's really been bugging me lately. I mean, it's not like I see it. It's not like he's kneeling at the side of the bed flogging himself with a leather switch or anything. I wish, right? No, it's more like he feels dirty and silently asks for forgiveness. And it's not like it's all the time either. In fact, he hardly ever does it. But still, it's like, really? That's what you have to do? I mean, all the other stuff I can sort of deal with, but the praying after sex? It just sort of makes everything feel a little tainted somehow. I mean, how am I gonna feel loved for real with, you know, all that in the way? *(Adam slugs back the rest of his cappuccino.)* Okay, I'll stop ... You talk ... If you want to. I know I'm sort of dumping this all out there, so ... But, please. If you have any ... pearls ... I'd be glad for anything. *(Brandon looks like Adam just puked all over him. He takes a moment to gather his thoughts, then speaks.)*

BRANDON. I like black men.

ADAM. Excuse me?

BRANDON. Black men?

ADAM. Uh-huh.

BRANDON. I like them ... That's all I've ever been attracted to ... I don't know why, it just is.

ADAM. Men that are black.

BRANDON. Yes.

ADAM. *(Unsure where this is headed.)* And you're telling me this because ...

BRANDON. Luke's not black.

ADAM. I see.

BRANDON. I was never in love with him, Adam. Our friendship ended because we both chose for it to. There was nothing "unrequited" about it.

ADAM. Gotcha.

BRANDON. I've been struggling with this stuff my whole life. When I met Luke, it was like, finally someone who understood. Finally someone I felt safe with. But somewhere along the line things started to shift. When you two were just hooking up, it was one thing, but when it turned into something, well, more ... Look, I understand the need to act on the urges, believe me, but to choose the lifestyle? To live like it was ... right, I guess? Well, that's where we go our separate ways.

ADAM. So, you're saying there was a line and, at a certain point,

Luke crossed it?

BRANDON. Moved it.

ADAM. So, it's okay to do ... whatever it is you do ... but when it comes to actually loving, that's where the line's drawn?

BRANDON. My line.

ADAM. At love? You draw your line at love, Brandon? Loving is too much of a sin?

BRANDON. If that's how you want to see it.

ADAM. That's not how I want to see it. That's not how I want anyone to see it. And I can't imagine that's how God wants us to see it either.

BRANDON. Well, it's how I see it. And Luke understands that. It took us a while, but we've made our peace. *(A beat.)*

ADAM. What about that guy in the chat room?

BRANDON. What guy?

ADAM. The married one ... Luke told me you really liked each other.

BRANDON. *(This stings.)* Oh, yeah? What else did he tell you?

ADAM. That he misses you.

BRANDON. *(This stings even more.)* Well, I miss him, too. And I'm sorry I can't support the two of you together. It just doesn't feel right. *(Brandon stands.)* So, I don't think I can help with the whole praying-after-sex thing.

ADAM. I guess not.

BRANDON. Give him my love, will you?

ADAM. You sure that's allowed? Not gonna get struck by lightning or anything, are you?

BRANDON. *(Genuine.)* You're funny, Adam. I'll give you that. I wish we could've gotten to know each other better, too.

ADAM. Oh, well. Maybe in our next life. Oops. Sorry. Guess not. *(A beat.)*

BRANDON. I don't know if this helps any, but ... he chose you, Adam. When he moved the line. That's got to have cost him, you know? And maybe praying after sex is the price he has to pay.

ADAM. Maybe.

BRANDON. Still ... He chose you ... Isn't that enough? *(Brandon leaves Adam alone to contemplate.)*

Scene 6

Luke's hospital room. The fluorescent lights are off. Adam's asleep, curled up against Luke. All is quiet except for the eerie sound of a machine that breathes.

After a few moments, the door opens. Adam wakes with a start, sitting bolt upright as Butch flips the lights on.

BUTCH. What's going on in here?

ADAM. Oh ... I ... uh ...

BUTCH. That's a hospital bed, son.

ADAM. Must have ...

BUTCH. I know you're jetlagged, but ... *(Adam hops off the bed, a little disoriented.)*

ADAM. What time is it?

BUTCH. A little after three.

ADAM. Brandon said you were getting a hotel room?

BUTCH. Couldn't sleep. *(Butch walks over and examines the machinery.)* Didn't mess anything up over here, did you? These things are ...

ADAM. I don't think so.

BUTCH. You sure? One flip of the switch and the whole thing can just ... *(Realizing he has no idea what he's talking about, Butch slumps down on the edge of the bed. He looks like an old man suddenly.)* There's a mother of three in Pennsylvania. Won't make it through the next twenty-four hours without a heart. *(He smooths his son's covers.)* A pair of eyes to Albany. A kidney to White Plains. Everyone needs something.

ADAM. Yeah ... *(The machine breathes.)*

BUTCH. You wanna make sure you're doing the right thing ... You look for some kind of sign ... Something to let you know ... And then ... Just like that ... *(Butch looks up at Adam.)* New Hope.

ADAM. Excuse me?

BUTCH. That's where she's from ... The mother ... Ironic, isn't it? *(He looks back down at his son.)* If you don't mind, I'd like to be alone with him. *(Adam doesn't move.)*

ADAM. Um …

BUTCH. Yes?

ADAM. I'm not quite done yet.

BUTCH. What's that?

ADAM. I'd like a little more time, if that's alright.

BUTCH. Time?

ADAM. If that's alright, yeah. *(Arlene enters, sensing trouble.)*

ARLENE. What's going on, fellas?

BUTCH. He wants time, Arlene. With Luke. He wants more of it.

ARLENE. Time?

ADAM. It's not … under the circumstances … I don't think that's a lot to ask. *(Butch slowly rises.)*

BUTCH. Is that right?

ADAM. Look, I don't wanna play this game anymore.

BUTCH. What game?

ADAM. You know what I'm talking about.

BUTCH. There's a game?

ADAM. Yes, and I'm not playing it.

ARLENE. Butch, maybe we should —

BUTCH. I wasn't aware of any game, Arlene, were you?

ADAM. Ten minutes … Just give me ten more minutes and I'll be out of here.

BUTCH. Ten minutes?

ARLENE. Come on, Butch. We can —

BUTCH. I'm not going anywhere.

ADAM. *(Exploding.)* I WANT MORE TIME, ALRIGHT!? I'M NOT ASKING ANYMORE, I'M TELLING YOU. *(Holly rushes in from the hallway.)* Now, I've been trying to be decent about all of this, but none of you are making it easy.

BUTCH. Who the heck is this guy?

ARLENE. Butch, please.

BUTCH. Walking in here like he owns the place.

ARLENE. Let's just —

BUTCH. I don't even know who you are, son.

ADAM. You don't know who I am?

HOLLY. Okay, everybody —

BUTCH. I could have your ass thrown out of here.

ADAM. I'm sure you could.

BUTCH. And there wouldn't be a damn thing you could do

about it.

HOLLY. Sweetie, maybe we should —

BUTCH. Coming in here, disrupting my family.

ARLENE. Okay, now. Stop it, Butch.

BUTCH. You've got a lot of nerve, son.

ADAM. I'm not your son.

BUTCH. No, you're not, are you? *(Just as it looks like the two men are about to strangle each other, Luke opens his eyes.)*

HOLLY. *(Gasping.)* Adam?! *(He's staring right at Adam. Adam is speechless.)*

ARLENE. Luke? *(Arlene leans in and touches her son's face.)* Can you hear me? It's me, Luke. It's Mama. *(Then, just as quickly, Luke's eyes close again.)*

BUTCH. Someone get a doctor.

ARLENE. Luke? Sweetheart? *(Holly runs off, leaving Adam there, frozen.)*

Scene 7

Adam's apartment. Yesterday. A weekend bag rests on the coffee table.

ADAM. *(Offstage.)* Is there anything I own that doesn't make me look like a lesbian from Scranton? *(Adam enters with a pile of clothes, and starts sorting through them.)* I mean, seriously. Since when did I start dressing like Paula Poundstone? *(Luke enters with a deli sandwich.)*

LUKE. Where's my cat?

ADAM. I have no idea.

LUKE. She was in here a minute ago.

ADAM. The vet said we shouldn't get too close. He's radioactive.

LUKE. For the first few days. It's been over a week.

ADAM. I'm not taking any chances.

LUKE. Adam!

ADAM. He's in the bathroom.

LUKE. She's not a he, you animal! *(Luke puts his sandwich down and heads for the bathroom.)* Patches?

ADAM. Did I snore again last night?

LUKE. *(Offstage.)* Like a buzz saw.

ADAM.   God, I'm becoming my father. I always thought I'd become my mother.

LUKE. *(Offstage.)* You got her hips. *(Luke reenters.)* You should see her. All curled up like a biscuit sandwich in there.

ADAM. You sure you can't come, babe? I've got a ton of miles I can cash in.

LUKE. Positive.

ADAM. It would just be so much more fun if you were there. I'm staying at my brother's, and you — *(Luke's dying to eat, but needs to pray first. Adam sees this, gives him his moment, then continues, a shorthand between them now.)* I'm staying at my brother's, and you love my brother.

LUKE. Believe me, there's nothing I'd rather do than sit around with a bunch of old farts comparing salaries all weekend.

ADAM. And hairlines. And potbellies.

LUKE. I'd love that, really I would. But I've got a ton of auditions this week. I'll go to your next reunion, I promise. I'll push your wheelchair.

ADAM. Fine, then don't forget to recycle when I'm gone. I mean it. I'm tired of seeing your Dr Pepper cans in the trash.

LUKE. Alright, already. Jeez, what crawled up your ass?

ADAM. Sorry, I'm just a little testy about having to fly in a hurricane.

LUKE. What hurricane?

ADAM. I don't know. There must be some hurricane heading our way. Don't we get them once a week now, thanks to you and all your ozone-eating Republican friends?

LUKE. George Bush did more for the EPA than Bill Clinton.

ADAM. Says who?

LUKE. I don't know. I read it.

ADAM. Where, in the Bible? *(Luke chuckles.)* You've ruined air travel for me, you know? Ever since you taught me about the Rapture, I start flop sweating if the pilot wears a cross or speaks with a Southern accent.

LUKE. Well, you know the solution.

ADAM. Yeah. Fly El-Al.

LUKE. Okay, Buster, but don't say I didn't warn you. *(Adam gives him a sweet kiss.)*

ADAM. Why would I need Jesus to save me when you already did?

LUKE. What's that thing on your face?

ADAM. What thing?

LUKE. That line thing.

ADAM. It's still there? *(Adam drops everything and runs to the mirror.)*

LUKE. What is it?

ADAM. A bed crease. I woke up with the fucking thing like five hours ago.

LUKE. So?

ADAM. So?! That didn't happen in my thirties. I'd wake up, and an hour later my face would spring back to normal. I've had this goddamn thing on my face for half a day now. *(Luke cracks up.)* It's not funny. Someday, you'll look back, ten, fifteen years from now, when you've moved on to someone else —

LUKE. Someone more age appropriate.

ADAM. Yes ... And you'll get a crease that takes half a day to go away, and your heart will break for me.

LUKE. And where will you be when that happens?

ADAM. Dead. *(Adam throws some more stuff into the bag.)* Wrong. Wrong. Wrong. *(He collapses dramatically on the couch.)* Please submit me for one of those makeover shows. I am begging you. *(Luke pulls the sweater we've seen Adam wearing in the waiting room scenes out of the pile.)*

LUKE. Here, wear this. You always look so handsome in periwinkle.

ADAM. Thanks. *(He helps Adam pull it on.)* I can't believe I'm going to this thing.

LUKE. It's just a reunion, babe. What's the big deal?

ADAM. What's the big deal?

LUKE. Oh, my God. You just vamped. You haven't done that in ages. You must really be freaked out.

ADAM. It's just ... This is the first time I'm going back as a teacher. Before, I was a writer. Not a very successful one, but still ... It just feels like a bit of a disappointment, that's all ... Like I've let the home team down.

LUKE. You're gonna look ten years younger than all of them.

ADAM. My body maybe, but not the rest of me. I've got lines and creases. My hair's dry. It doesn't shine anymore. It's like someone cut an old man's head off and stuck it on a young man's torso. It's unnatural.

LUKE. Would you stop.

ADAM. I should either stop with the treadmill, and let myself go completely, or cash in my IRA and get a face, brow and a neck lift.

LUKE. You don't need a neck lift. *(Adam glares at him playfully as he zips up his bag.)*

ADAM. Okay, I'm outta here.

LUKE. Will you crack my back before you go?

ADAM. I don't like cracking.

LUKE. I bet the cute new stock boy at the candle shop does.

ADAM. You want it cracked or broken? *(Adam pushes Luke down on the couch. Luke puts his head in Adam's lap, and Adam starts cracking.)*

LUKE. No, not like that … Yeah … A little higher. *(Adam spots something.)*

ADAM. Is that a gray hair?

LUKE. Where?

ADAM. It is! Oh, my God! Thank you, Jesus! *(Luke tries to break free, but Adam starts tickling him. The playful wrestling eventually subsides, until they're lying on top of each other, out of breath and totally in love.)* I don't want to go. *(Luke wraps his arms around Adam.)*

LUKE. I love you.

ADAM. I know you do.

LUKE. *(Sensing hesitation.)* But?

ADAM. *(Sheepish.)* I want you to love me more than Him. *(Luke grins.)* I'm serious. *(The grin disappears.)*

LUKE. I know you are. *(Luke pushes Adam off. They both sit up, on opposite sides of the couch. The divide between them, once again, seemingly insurmountable. They sit there in silence for a moment.)*

ADAM. Did you ever think that maybe you were the crazy one?

LUKE. Not really, no … Once, maybe … for a moment … but then, you know … *(Some muffled music from the apartment above.)*

ADAM. The NYU kids are back … From summer.

LUKE. Yeah.

ADAM. How long's your brother been at Georgia Tech? He's a sophomore now, right?

LUKE. Uh-huh.

ADAM. *(An epiphany.)* It's never gonna change, is it? *(A beat.)*

LUKE. I'm not sure. *(They sit there a minute longer, one looking more miserable than the other, until Adam rises, grabs his weekend bag, and walks to the door.)*

ADAM. I don't think I can do this anymore. *(And with that, he walks out the door, leaving Luke sitting there as the NYU kids grow louder.)*

Scene 8

The waiting room. Brandon and Holly sit side by side. The mood is somber, reverent.

HOLLY. Have you ever sat shiva, Brandon?

BRANDON. No.

HOLLY. Wonder if this is what it feels like.

BRANDON. I'm not even really sure what shiva is.

HOLLY. Me neither. *(Arlene and Butch enter. Adam's not far behind. Arlene walks to the couch and sits next to Holly. She has a certain peace about her. Butch doesn't. Holly looks at Adam. He seems miles away.)*

ARLENE. So ... That's it. He's ... It's ... over. *(Arlene takes hold of Holly's hand.)* I keep thinking about that play Luke was in, Brandon. That *Our Town*. Little images keep popping into my head. An ice cream parlor. Two giant step ladders. A cemetery made of chairs. I remember there wasn't much scenery to speak of, but somehow they made you see everything.

HOLLY. It was a beautiful production.

ARLENE. Yes, it was. *(A long silence.)* But I can't quite remember what it was about. *(Holly and Brandon exchange a glance.)*

HOLLY. Well, there was this girl in a small New England town.

ARLENE. Back in the olden days, right. I remember that.

HOLLY. Uh-huh. And she dies. Gets consumption, or dies in childbirth or something, which happened a lot back in those days, I guess, and just ... dies. But she's allowed to go back and revisit one day of her life, and all the people she loved. And she's feeling so much for them. Because she's ... But they don't know she is, and they take her for granted. And each other. And she sees how sad that is ... and was ... even before she died, and she wonders if anyone ever realizes how wonderful life is. How precious. Even as they're living it. *(A beat.)*

ARLENE. That's right. Now, I remember. *(Arlene looks to Butch.)* Butch?

BUTCH. They take the organs out before they pull the plug ... I never knew that.

ARLENE. Why don't you come sit with us?

69

BUTCH. Pack it all up in little coolers ... Like they're off to a picnic or something.

ARLENE. Sweetheart?

BUTCH. I can't feel anything, Arlene.

ARLENE. Come here, hon.

BUTCH. My fingers ... My arm ...

ARLENE. Butch ...

BUTCH. They keep it so damn cold in here. How's anyone supposed to ...

ARLENE. Do you want me to get the pastor?

BUTCH. The pastor? No, I don't think I want a pastor right now.

ARLENE. How about a walk then? Maybe we should go for a walk, hon. Just you and me. How about that? *(Butch looks down the hallway.)*

BUTCH. Another blanket ... He needs another ...

ARLENE. Sweetheart? *(He starts towards Luke's room, stopping when he realizes Luke's no longer there. He lingers for a moment, then collapses out of nowhere. Adam is able to catch him before he hits the ground. Everyone is stunned. Butch more so than anyone else. Together, he and Adam look like some sort of strange* Pietà. *He lays there, completely confused for a moment, then hides his face in Adam's chest and begins to weep. Adam looks at the others, unsure what to do, until, finally, he finds some inspiration for all of them.)*

ADAM. Luke wasn't afraid. That's what he told me. He said the place he was going was gonna be so beautiful. He was certain of it. And he knew ... that everyone he loved ... most everyone ... would, one day, be there with him. *(Adam's words seem to provide some momentary comfort. Butch slowly pulls himself together, rises to his feet, and stares at him.)*

BUTCH. Carl Randolph.

ADAM. Excuse me?

BUTCH. The day I got my books. That's how I know you. Couldn't figure it out at first, but ...

ARLENE. Why don't we get out of here for a little while, Butch? Go for a walk or something. We'll come back and deal with all the ... with everything later.

BUTCH. A drink.

ARLENE. Whatever it takes.

BRANDON. There's a place around the corner.

ARLENE. Around the corner?

BRANDON. I'll show you.

ARLENE. Thank you, Brandon. *(Holly hands Brandon his jacket.)*

BRANDON. I'll call you later.

HOLLY. Okay. *(They hug. Arlene scribbles something on the back of a card as Butch wanders slowly out of the room.)*

ARLENE. Would you go grab him, Brandon? I'll meet you at the elevator. *(Brandon gives Adam's shoulder a squeeze on his way out. Arlene tears off a piece of the* Newsweek *and scribbles her number on it.)* This is my cell. Not sure where we'll be tonight, but please call. There's a lot to take care of, and I know I'm gonna need help. *(She hands it to Holly, then moves on to Adam and hugs him for an uncomfortably long time.)* You, too. *(She lets go of him and scoots out of the room. Adam and Holly just stand there. The buzz of the fluorescents is deafening.)*

ADAM. He looked at me.

HOLLY. He did, sweetie.

ADAM. He opened his eyes and just … looked at me.

HOLLY. Adam, I'm … I'm so …

ADAM. It happens, I guess, that's what the nurse told me … People wake up sometimes … for a minute or two just before they go … almost like they know. *(A beat.)* And, you know, all the doubts, everything I've been questioning for the past five years, none of it meant anything, all of a sudden. It was just us … Me and Luke … That's all that mattered … *(Another beat.)* And it was like … *finally* … I believed. *(Holly squeezes Adam's hand.)* I keep thinking about yesterday. Before I left for the airport. I can't remember if we said goodbye. *(He starts to crumble.)* I want to go.

HOLLY. With them?

ADAM. No. Home. Your place. Anywhere.

HOLLY. Okay. Let me just … get our stuff. *(Holly starts gathering their things.)* Brandon left his Bible. *(She picks up the Bible, and stuffs it into her bag.)* God, this thing is so … worn out. *(Adam keeps looking around the room like he's forgotten something.)* Are you ready, sweetie?

ADAM. Am I ready? *(A phone rings. Confused, Holly follows the sound of the ring over to the couch and digs out a cell phone.)*

HOLLY. Must be Butch's. *(She hands it over. Adam looks at the caller ID.)*

ADAM. It's Ben … Luke's brother. *(Unsure what to do, he stares at the phone, then flips it open, and speaks.)* Hello … Oh … uh … No. This is … um … *(He looks at Holly.)* My name's Adam. *(Lights slowly fade to black.)*

End of Play

PROPERTY LIST

Kleenex box, magazines
Old book
Cups of coffee
Medical forms
3 cell phones
Wet jacket
Glass of water
Postcard
Kleenex or hankie
Newsweek magazine (prehistoric man cover)
Cup of coffee
Lady's coat and purse
Pill bottle
Plate of fried eggs, tomatoes, coffee
Coffee pot
Chinese takeout
Housewarming gift
Unopened boxes
Bottle of wine, 3 glasses
Orange candle
Wristwatch
Deck of cards
Junk in closet
Coat
Books
Tinky Winky doll
Framed photos
Breakaway-bottom box
2 cups of tea
Honey bear
Windex
Laptop
Sleeping pills
Bible
Bowl of yarmulkes, prayer shawls
2 cups boutique coffee
Weekend bag
Pile of clothes

Deli sandwich
Sweater
Jacket
Pen and bit of paper

SOUND EFFECTS

Brakes squeal to a halt, followed by stuck car horn
Low buzz of fluorescent lighting
Loud crash
Teakettle whistle
Toilet flush
Breathing machine
Muffled music from above
Phone ring

NEW PLAYS

★ **MOTHERHOOD OUT LOUD by Leslie Ayvazian, Brooke Berman, David Cale, Jessica Goldberg, Beth Henley, Lameece Issaq, Claire LaZebnik, Lisa Loomer, Michele Lowe, Marco Pennette, Theresa Rebeck, Luanne Rice, Annie Weisman and Cheryl L. West, conceived by Susan R. Rose and Joan Stein.** When entrusting the subject of motherhood to such a dazzling collection of celebrated American writers, what results is a joyous, moving, hilarious, and altogether thrilling theatrical event. "Never fails to strike both the funny bone and the heart." –*BackStage*. "Packed with wisdom, laughter, and plenty of wry surprises." –*TheaterMania*. [1M, 3W] ISBN: 978-0-8222-2589-8

★ **COCK by Mike Bartlett.** When John takes a break from his boyfriend, he accidentally meets the girl of his dreams. Filled with guilt and indecision, he decides there is only one way to straighten this out. "[A] brilliant and blackly hilarious feat of provocation." –*Independent*. "A smart, prickly and rewarding view of sexual and emotional confusion." –*Evening Standard*. [3M, 1W] ISBN: 978-0-8222-2766-3

★ **F. Scott Fitzgerald's THE GREAT GATSBY adapted for the stage by Simon Levy.** Jay Gatsby, a self-made millionaire, passionately pursues the elusive Daisy Buchanan. Nick Carraway, a young newcomer to Long Island, is drawn into their world of obsession, greed and danger. "Levy's combination of narration, dialogue and action delivers most of what is best in the novel." –*Seattle Post-Intelligencer*. "A beautifully crafted interpretation of the 1925 novel which defined the Jazz Age." –*London Free Press*. [5M, 4W] ISBN: 978-0-8222-2727-4

★ **LONELY, I'M NOT by Paul Weitz.** At an age when most people are discovering what they want to do with their lives, Porter has been married and divorced, earned seven figures as a corporate "ninja," and had a nervous breakdown. It's been four years since he's had a job or a date, and he's decided to give life another shot. "Critic's pick!" –*NY Times*. "An enjoyable ride." –*NY Daily News*. [3M, 3W] ISBN: 978-0-8222-2734-2

★ **ASUNCION by Jesse Eisenberg.** Edgar and Vinny are not racist. In fact, Edgar maintains a blog condemning American imperialism, and Vinny is three-quarters into a Ph.D. in Black Studies. When Asuncion becomes their new roommate, the boys have a perfect opportunity to demonstrate how open-minded they truly are. "Mr. Eisenberg writes lively dialogue that strikes plenty of comic sparks." –*NY Times*. "An almost ridiculously enjoyable portrait of slacker trauma among would-be intellectuals." –*Newsday*. [2M, 2W] ISBN: 978-0-8222-2630-7

DRAMATISTS PLAY SERVICE, INC.
440 Park Avenue South, New York, NY 10016   212-683-8960   Fax 212-213-1539
postmaster@dramatists.com   www.dramatists.com

NEW PLAYS

★ **THE PICTURE OF DORIAN GRAY by Roberto Aguirre-Sacasa, based on the novel by Oscar Wilde.** Preternaturally handsome Dorian Gray has his portrait painted by his college classmate Basil Hallwood. When their mutual friend Henry Wotton offers to include it in a show, Dorian makes a fateful wish—that his portrait should grow old instead of him—and strikes an unspeakable bargain with the devil. [5M, 2W] ISBN: 978-0-8222-2590-4

★ **THE LYONS by Nicky Silver.** As Ben Lyons lies dying, it becomes clear that he and his wife have been at war for many years, and his impending demise has brought no relief. When they're joined by their children all efforts at a sentimental goodbye to the dying patriarch are soon abandoned. "Hilariously frank, clear-sighted, compassionate and forgiving." –*NY Times.* "Mordant, dark and rich." –*Associated Press.* [3M, 3W] ISBN: 978-0-8222-2659-8

★ **STANDING ON CEREMONY by Mo Gaffney, Jordan Harrison, Moisés Kaufman, Neil LaBute, Wendy MacLeod, José Rivera, Paul Rudnick, and Doug Wright, conceived by Brian Shnipper.** Witty, warm and occasionally wacky, these plays are vows to the blessings of equality, the universal challenges of relationships and the often hilarious power of love. "CEREMONY puts a human face on a hot-button issue and delivers laughter and tears rather than propaganda." –*BackStage.* [3M, 3W] ISBN: 978-0-8222-2654-3

★ **ONE ARM by Moisés Kaufman, based on the short story and screenplay by Tennessee Williams.** Ollie joins the Navy and becomes the lightweight boxing champion of the Pacific Fleet. Soon after, he loses his arm in a car accident, and he turns to hustling to survive. "[A] fast, fierce, brutally beautiful stage adaptation." –*NY Magazine.* "A fascinatingly lurid, provocative and fatalistic piece of theater." –*Variety.* [7M, 1W] ISBN: 978-0-8222-2564-5

★ **AN ILIAD by Lisa Peterson and Denis O'Hare.** A modern-day retelling of Homer's classic. Poetry and humor, the ancient tale of the Trojan War and the modern world collide in this captivating theatrical experience. "Shocking, glorious, primal and deeply satisfying." –*Time Out NY.* "Explosive, altogether breathtaking." –*Chicago Sun-Times.* [1M] ISBN: 978-0-8222-2687-1

★ **THE COLUMNIST by David Auburn.** At the height of the Cold War, Joe Alsop is the nation's most influential journalist, beloved, feared and courted by the Washington world. But as the '60s dawn and America undergoes dizzying change, the intense political dramas Joe is embroiled in become deeply personal as well. "Intensely satisfying." –*Bloomberg News.* [5M, 2W] ISBN: 978-0-8222-2699-4

DRAMATISTS PLAY SERVICE, INC.
440 Park Avenue South, New York, NY 10016   212-683-8960   Fax 212-213-1539
postmaster@dramatists.com   www.dramatists.com

NEW PLAYS

★ **BENGAL TIGER AT THE BAGHDAD ZOO by Rajiv Joseph.** The lives of two American Marines and an Iraqi translator are forever changed by an encounter with a quick-witted tiger who haunts the streets of war-torn Baghdad. "[A] boldly imagined, harrowing and surprisingly funny drama." *–NY Times.* "Tragic yet darkly comic and highly imaginative." *–CurtainUp.* [5M, 2W] ISBN: 978-0-8222-2565-2

★ **THE PITMEN PAINTERS by Lee Hall, inspired by a book by William Feaver.** Based on the triumphant true story, a group of British miners discover a new way to express themselves and unexpectedly become art-world sensations. "Excitingly ambiguous, in-the-moment theater." *–NY Times.* "Heartfelt, moving and deeply politicized." *–Chicago Tribune.* [5M, 2W] ISBN: 978-0-8222-2507-2

★ **RELATIVELY SPEAKING by Ethan Coen, Elaine May and Woody Allen.** In TALKING CURE, Ethan Coen uncovers the sort of insanity that can only come from family. Elaine May explores the hilarity of passing in GEORGE IS DEAD. In HONEYMOON MOTEL, Woody Allen invites you to the sort of wedding day you won't forget. "Firecracker funny." *–NY Times.* "A rollicking good time." *–New Yorker.* [8M, 7W] ISBN: 978-0-8222-2394-8

★ **SONS OF THE PROPHET by Stephen Karam.** If to live is to suffer, then Joseph Douaihy is more alive than most. With unexplained chronic pain and the fate of his reeling family on his shoulders, Joseph's health, sanity, and insurance premium are on the line. "Explosively funny." *–NY Times.* "At once deep, deft and beautifully made." *–New Yorker.* [5M, 3W] ISBN: 978-0-8222-2597-3

★ **THE MOUNTAINTOP by Katori Hall.** A gripping reimagination of events the night before the assassination of the civil rights leader Dr. Martin Luther King, Jr. "An ominous electricity crackles through the opening moments." *–NY Times.* "[A] thrilling, wild, provocative flight of magical realism." *–Associated Press.* "Crackles with theatricality and a humanity more moving than sainthood." *–NY Newsday.* [1M, 1W] ISBN: 978-0-8222-2603-1

★ **ALL NEW PEOPLE by Zach Braff.** Charlie is 35, heartbroken, and just wants some time away from the rest of the world. Long Beach Island seems to be the perfect escape until his solitude is interrupted by a motley parade of misfits who show up and change his plans. "Consistently and sometimes sensationally funny." *–NY Times.* "A morbidly funny play about the trendy new existential condition of being young, adorable, and miserable." *–Variety.* [2M, 2W] ISBN: 978-0-8222-2562-1

DRAMATISTS PLAY SERVICE, INC.
440 Park Avenue South, New York, NY 10016 212-683-8960 Fax 212-213-1539
postmaster@dramatists.com www.dramatists.com

NEW PLAYS

★ **CLYBOURNE PARK by Bruce Norris.** WINNER OF THE 2011 PULITZER PRIZE AND 2012 TONY AWARD. Act One takes place in 1959 as community leaders try to stop the sale of a home to a black family. Act Two is set in the same house in the present day as the now predominantly African-American neighborhood battles to hold its ground. "Vital, sharp-witted and ferociously smart." –*NY Times*. "A theatrical treasure…Indisputably, uproariously funny." –*Entertainment Weekly*. [4M, 3W] ISBN: 978-0-8222-2697-0

★ **WATER BY THE SPOONFUL by Quiara Alegría Hudes.** WINNER OF THE 2012 PULITZER PRIZE. A Puerto Rican veteran is surrounded by the North Philadelphia demons he tried to escape in the service. "This is a very funny, warm, and yes uplifting play." –*Hartford Courant*. "The play is a combination poem, prayer and app on how to cope in an age of uncertainty, speed and chaos." –*Variety*. [4M, 3W] ISBN: 978-0-8222-2716-8

★ **RED by John Logan.** WINNER OF THE 2010 TONY AWARD. Mark Rothko has just landed the biggest commission in the history of modern art. But when his young assistant, Ken, gains the confidence to challenge him, Rothko faces the agonizing possibility that his crowning achievement could also become his undoing. "Intense and exciting." –*NY Times*. "Smart, eloquent entertainment." –*New Yorker*. [2M] ISBN: 978-0-8222-2483-9

★ **VENUS IN FUR by David Ives.** Thomas, a beleaguered playwright/director, is desperate to find an actress to play Vanda, the female lead in his adaptation of the classic sadomasochistic tale *Venus in Fur*. "Ninety minutes of good, kinky fun." –*NY Times*. "A fast-paced journey into one man's entrapment by a clever, vengeful female." –*Associated Press*. [1M, 1W] ISBN: 978-0-8222-2603-1

★ **OTHER DESERT CITIES by Jon Robin Baitz.** Brooke returns home to Palm Springs after a six-year absence and announces that she is about to publish a memoir dredging up a pivotal and tragic event in the family's history—a wound they don't want reopened. "Leaves you feeling both moved and gratifyingly sated." –*NY Times*. "A genuine pleasure." –*NY Post*. [2M, 3W] ISBN: 978-0-8222-2605-5

★ **TRIBES by Nina Raine.** Billy was born deaf into a hearing family and adapts brilliantly to his family's unconventional ways, but it's not until he meets Sylvia, a young woman on the brink of deafness, that he finally understands what it means to be understood. "A smart, lively play." –*NY Times*. "[A] bright and boldly provocative drama." –*Associated Press*. [3M, 2W] ISBN: 978-0-8222-2751-9

DRAMATISTS PLAY SERVICE, INC.
440 Park Avenue South, New York, NY 10016 212-683-8960 Fax 212-213-1539
postmaster@dramatists.com www.dramatists.com